PASS THE
U.S. CITIZENSHIP
EXAM

PASS THE U.S. CITIZENSHIP EXAM

2011 UPDATE

4th Edition

LEARNINGEXPRESS®

NEW YORK

Library of Congress Cataloging-in-Publication Data:
 Pass the U.S. citizenship exam. — 4th ed.
     p. cm.
 ISBN-13: 978-1-57685-784-7
 ISBN-10: 1-57685-784-0
 1. Citizenship—United States—Examinations—Study guides. I. LearningExpress (Organization) II. Title: Pass the US citizenship exam. III. Title: Pass the United States citizenship exam.
 JK1758.M37 2011
 323.6'230973--dc22
                             2010028892

Printed in the United States of America

9 8 7 6 5 4 3 2

Fourth Edition

ISBN: 978-1-57685-784-7

For information on LearningExpress, other LearningExpress products, or bulk sales, please write to us at:
   2 Rector Street
   26th Floor
   New York, NY 10006

Or visit us at:
   www.learnatest.com

CONTENTS ▶

PASS THE U.S. CITIZENSHIP EXAM

HOW TO USE THIS BOOK ▶

This book is designed to help you pass the United States Citizenship Exam. It also explains the process of how to become a United States citizen. However, this book does not give legal advice. Go to your lawyer for help with immigration laws. You may want to study this book by yourself, with a partner, or in a formal classroom. The book is written for people whose first language is not English.

What You Will Find in This Book

There are three sections in this book. Section I—Chapters 1, 2, and 3—gives you a complete overview of the process of becoming a U.S. citizen. Chapter 1 offers information about the benefits and responsibilities that come with U.S. citizenship. You should know why you want to become a U.S. citizen. Chapter 2 explains what you need to do to become a U.S. citizen. Remember that naturalization laws can change. Ask your lawyer or someone from the U.S. Citizenship and Immigration Services (USCIS) for updated information. Chapter 3 shows you which USCIS regional office you should contact for more information or to send your completed N-400 application form.

Section II of this book—Chapters 4, 5, 6, and 7—covers the exam and 12 lessons, each with vocabulary words, relevant questions, and exercises. By the end of this section, you will have seen the entire list of 100 sample questions that you may be asked. After you study all the concepts, do the exercises at the end of each lesson to make sure you remember all the information. You will find the answers to the exercises and review tests at the end of Section II. Do not look at the answers until after you try to answer each question. At the end of each lesson, you will also find dictation practices. Dictation is when the USCIS person says a sentence out loud and you write it down.

Section III—Chapters 8, 9, and 10—will walk you through the steps of the actual citizenship interview. Each chapter covers a different stage of the interview process. Chapter 8 prepares you for the small talk, the truth oath, and the identity check. Chapter 9 helps familiarize you with the information on your N-400 form and discusses how your interviewer may ask you questions about your information. Chapter 10 goes over the questions that the interviewer may ask you on basic U.S. history and civics from the questions covered in Section II. Work slowly and carefully through each lesson, and practice all the exercises. The review at the end of Section III revisits some of the key concepts.

The appendix includes a sample copy of the N-400 Application for Naturalization for you to practice filling out. You will also find a list of useful websites and books to use as resources.

After reading and studying this book, you will be well on your way to passing the U.S. Citizenship Exam. Good luck!

Study for Success!

You will have the most success from using this book and studying for the U.S. Citizenship Exam by:

- finding a quiet location to work
- using good light to prep
- turning off the television and computer, and avoiding any other distractions
- organizing an effective study group

Set realistic study goals and a prep schedule—and stick to them!

SECTION

PROCESS OVERVIEW

1 ▶ WHAT IS CITIZENSHIP?

Since its founding over 200 years ago, America has stood for the ideals of democracy, independence, and freedom. Every year, hundreds of thousands of people come to America seeking new opportunities in this "land of the free" and "home of the brave." Many of these immigrants take the final step in making America their new home by becoming U.S. citizens. Do you want to take this step? Before you decide to become an American citizen, you should be aware of the benefits and responsibilities of citizenship.

Benefits of Citizenship
- You get the right to vote in elections.
- You get to run for certain public offices.
- You get to apply for jobs with the government.
- You get to ask for your close family members to come to America legally.
- Your family members may get to come to America more quickly.
- More of your family members may get to come to America.
- Your unmarried children may become citizens.

- You may get Social Security benefits even if you live in another country.
- You get to live outside the United States without losing your citizenship.
- You get to travel with a U.S. passport.
- You get to reenter the United States more easily.
- You don't have to renew a green card.
- You don't have to report a change of address.
- You will not be deported.
- You get more benefits from the government.
- You don't have to worry about new immigration laws.

Responsibilities of Citizenship

- You must take an Oath of Allegiance to America.
- You can participate in government by voting in elections.

However, the most important reason to become a U.S. citizen is if you identify with American ideals and you love America. This book will give you a basic understanding of U.S. civics and history, as well as a review of the USCIS interview format, so that you can pass the U.S. Citizenship Exam and become an American citizen.

Practice

Think about the reasons why you want to become an American citizen, because you may need to answer this question in your USCIS interview:

Why do you want to become a United States citizen?

THE PROCESS OF BECOMING A CITIZEN

This chapter will show you how you can become a U.S. citizen. There are many steps to this process and it may take several months to complete all the steps. The best way to prepare for the process of becoming a citizen is to know what to expect. Read this chapter carefully. See the flowchart on the following page for an overview of the process.

Citizenship Process

The process usually takes an average of six to nine months, according to USCIS. Be sure to submit all the correct documents that USCIS requests.

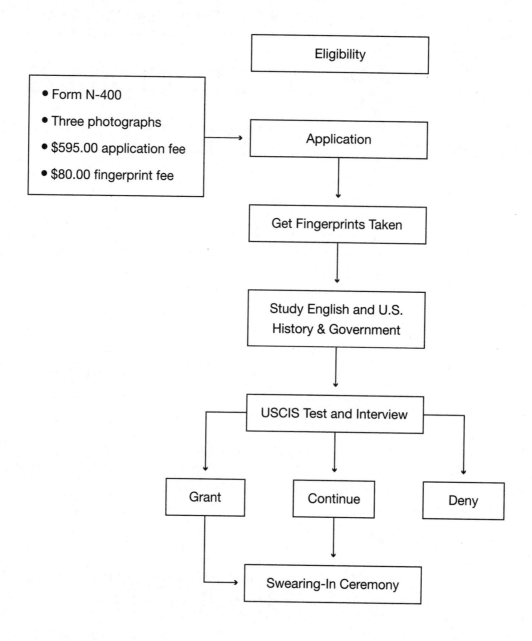

Eligibility Quiz

Find out if you are ready to apply for U.S. citizenship. Circle either **Yes** or **No**.

Yes No Are you at least 18 years old?

Yes No Have you been a lawful permanent resident of the United States either for five years, OR for three years if you have been married for three years to a person who has been a U.S. citizen for at least three years?

Yes No During the past five years, have you been physically present in the United States for at least $2\frac{1}{2}$ years (30 months), OR $1\frac{1}{2}$ years (18 months) if you are married to a U.S. citizen?

Yes No Have you lived within the state or district in which you currently reside for at least three months?

Yes No Do you have good moral character?

Yes No Can you read, write, and speak simple English?

Yes No Do you know about U.S. government and history?

Yes No Are you willing to swear loyalty to the United States?

If you circled **Yes** to all of the questions, you are ready to apply to become a U.S. citizen. If you answered **No** to any of the questions, ask an immigration specialist if you are ready. There are special reasons for answering **No**, and you may still be able to apply to become a U.S. citizen.

The Application

You need to submit an application called the N-400 Application for Naturalization to the USCIS. You also have to submit three photographs of yourself and a money order, personal check, or cashier's check for the application and fingerprint fee (when this book was made, the application fee was $595 plus an $80 fingerprint fee). The fees may be paid in one check (total of the check is $675). Applicants 75 years of age or older are not charged a finger print fee. Their total fee is $595. Make the check payable to the U.S. Citizenship and Immigration Services.

Send These to the USCIS

- Form N-400
- Three photographs
- One check for the total fee, made payable to U.S. Citizenship and Immigration Services

You can get the N-400 application from a USCIS office near you. Visit the USCIS website at www.uscis.gov or call 1-800-375-5283 to find your local USCIS office. Then you can do one of the following:

- Write them a letter to ask for the form.
- Go to the office and pick up the form.
- Call them on the phone and ask for the form.
- Download and print the forms at www.uscis.gov.

Tell the truth when you fill out the N-400 application form. Get help if you need it. See Chapter 3 for where to find help.

Tips for Assembling Your Application

- Print clearly with black ink or type your answers.
- Check your application for spelling errors.
- Check your application to be sure that you have completed all of the items on the form.
- Before inserting your application into a mailing envelope, make copies of every page for your records.
- Gather all necessary supporting documents and include copies.
- Keep all copies and material in a safe place, for future reference.
- Follow the instructions for submitting payment—do not send cash.
- Clearly mark both the envelope and your cover letter with the form type: *N-400 Application for Naturalization.*
- Use the correct mailing address.

Fingerprints

Do not send a fingerprint card with your N-400 application. After the USCIS receives your N-400 application, they will send you an appointment letter with the address of the nearest USCIS-authorized fingerprint site. Read the instructions in the appointment letter. Take the letter to the USCIS-authorized fingerprint site when you go to your fingerprint appointment. After you get your fingerprints taken, mail any additional documents that the USCIS might request and wait for them to schedule your interview.

Study

Read and study this book and any other material that will help you understand U.S. government and history. You need to know the material included in this book. You may also want to take a class on how to pass the U.S. Citizenship Exam.

The Test

The USCIS will test you about U.S. government and history during your interview. They will ask you questions in English and you will answer them out loud in English. During the interview, you will also need to write down one or two sentences that you hear. To pass the test, you must answer 60% of the questions correctly. If you do not pass the test, you will get one more try. If you do not pass the test the second time, you will have to start the whole process over and wait another several months to get a new interview date.

Three Important Exceptions

You can take the test in your native language (not English) if you are:
- Fifty-five years old and have lived in America for 15 years as a lawful permanent resident

OR

- Fifty years old and have lived in America for 20 years as a lawful permanent resident

You can take an easier test in your native language if you are:
- Sixty-five years old and have lived in America for 20 years as a lawful permanent resident

The Interview

You will be given a date to go for your USCIS interview. It may take 10–12 months to get a date for the interview. Be sure to attend your interview on the date you are given. If you must miss your interview, you should contact the office where your interview is scheduled as soon as possible, asking to reschedule your interview. At the interview, you must promise to tell the truth by taking an oath. You will be asked questions about your N-400 application. You will also be asked questions about yourself, your children, your work, and your life. You must answer these questions in English. If you have a physical, mental, or developmental disability, talk to an immigration specialist to find out if you can avoid speaking English and answering questions about the American government during the interview.

Swearing-In Ceremony

If you pass the test and the interview, you will get a letter within two months. The letter will tell you the date and time of a swearing-in ceremony. At the ceremony, you will take the Oath of Allegiance (say that you are loyal to the United States) and exchange your permanent residency card for a U.S. citizenship certificate. After the ceremony, you will be an American citizen.

The USCIS office may also continue your case. If your case is continued, it will add time to your naturalization process. The most common reasons for continuation are (1) failing the English and civics tests and/or (2) failing to give the USCIS the needed documents. If your case is continued, you will be asked to either come to a second interview or to provide additional documents. If you do not do what the USCIS requires, your application may be denied. If your application is denied, you will receive a written notice telling you why. If you feel that you have been wrongly denied citizenship, you may request a hearing with a USCIS officer. Your denial letter will explain how to request a hearing and will include the form you need.

HOW AND WHERE TO GET HELP

You can find help in becoming a U.S. citizen in many places. This chapter includes contact information for the USCIS lockbox facilities so you can find the one for your state. Other groups offer help too, and this chapter includes information on how to access that help.

USCIS Lockbox Facilities

Here is a list of where to send your completed N-400 Application for Naturalization form. There are two regional USCIS lockbox facilities. Look for your state and then send your N-400 application to the address that appears after your state.

Be sure to keep a copy of everything you send to USCIS.

If you live in one of these states:

Alaska	Michigan	Utah
Arizona	Minnesota	Washington
California	Missouri	Wisconsin
Colorado	Montana	Wyoming
Hawaii	Nebraska	OR
Idaho	Nevada	Territory of Guam
Illinois	North Dakota	Commonwealth of the Northern
Indiana	Ohio	Mariana Islands
Iowa	Oregon	
Kansas	South Dakota	

Then send your completed N-400 application form to this address:

USCIS
P.O. Box 21251
Phoenix, AZ 85036

If you live in one of these states:

Alabama	Massachusetts	South Carolina
Arkansas	Mississippi	Tennessee
Connecticut	New Hampshire	Texas
Delaware	New Jersey	Vermont
Florida	New Mexico	Virginia
Georgia	New York	Washington, D.C.
Kentucky	North Carolina	West Virginia
Louisiana	Oklahoma	OR
Maine	Pennsylvania	Commonwealth of Puerto Rico
Maryland	Rhode Island	U.S. Virgin Islands

Then send your completed N-400 application form to this address:

USCIS
P.O. Box 660060
Dallas, TX 75266

USCIS Service Center for Military Members and Spouses

If you are filing an application under military provisions, then send your completed N-400 application to this address (regardless of where you live and whether you are filing from within the U.S. or abroad):

Nebraska Service Center
P.O. Box 87426
Lincoln, NE 68501-7426

USCIS Help

USCIS offers a customer service phone line to assist you during the naturalization process. To access this service, call 1-800-375-5283. There is no fee for the USCIS customer service.

Legal Help

You may want to pay for an attorney to help you complete the N-400 Application for Naturalization form. If so, look in your phone book for the phone number of your state's bar association or the Legal Aid Society. Many immigration attorneys also advertise in the yellow pages of the phone book. Be careful when you choose an attorney. Ask friends or relatives to suggest an attorney if they know of a good one.

One place you can contact for more information is the American Immigration Lawyers Association (AILA). It has over 10,000 attorneys who practice immigration law. AILA Member attorneys represent tens of thousands of U.S. families who have applied for permanent residence for their spouses, children, and other close relatives to lawfully enter and reside in the United States. You can ask for a referral to an immigration attorney by contacting them at:

American Immigration Lawyers Association
918 F Street, NW
Washington, D.C. 20004-1400
202-216-2400
www.aila.org

Community-Based Resources

Many local libraries and state governments offer free courses that help qualified candidates through the entire naturalization process, including preparation for the U.S. Citizenship Exam. Check with your local library and government to see what they offer. In addition, there are many national and community-based organizations that assist candidates with everything from exam preparation to legal services for free or low cost. Ask your local librarian to assist you with finding these organizations. You can also search the Internet using the following search terms alone or in combination, including your home state or city: *naturalization assistance*, *citizenship assistance*, *naturalization programs*, and *citizenship programs*.

THE 100 QUESTIONS

The next four chapters will help you prepare for the exam, using the LearningExpress Test Preparation System and reviewing the U.S. civics, history, and government concepts that you may be tested on at your citizenship interview. Chapters 5, 6, and 7 cover several lessons, with vocabulary words, relevant questions, and exercises. Work slowly and carefully through each lesson, and complete all the exercises. The section review at the end of the section revisits some of these key concepts. At the end of this section, you'll find a list of 100 questions. These 100 questions comprise the entire body of information that might appear on your citizenship test. Study these questions and you will be very prepared for the test. The answers to the exercises can be found starting on page 107.

Here's an outline of what's in this section:

THE LEARNINGEXPRESS TEST PREPARATION SYSTEM

CHAPTER OVERVIEW

Taking any exam can be tough. It demands a lot of preparation if you want to pass the U.S. Citizenship Exam. The LearningExpress Test Preparation System, developed exclusively for LearningExpress by leading test experts, gives you the discipline and attitude you need to achieve your dream of becoming a U.S. citizen.

Taking this exam is a challenge, and so is getting ready for it. Your potential status as a citizen depends on passing the exam, but there are all sorts of pitfalls that can keep you from doing your best. Here are some of the obstacles that can stand in the way of your success:

- being unfamiliar with the format of the exam
- being paralyzed by test anxiety
- leaving your preparation to the last minute or not preparing at all
- not being in tip-top mental and physical shape
- messing up on test day by having to work on an empty stomach or shivering through the exam because the room is cold

What's the common denominator in all these test-taking pitfalls? One word: control. Who's in control, you or the exam?

Here's the good news: The LearningExpress Test Preparation System puts you in control. In just six easy-to-follow steps, you will learn everything you need to know to make sure that you are in charge of your preparation and your performance on the exam. Other test-takers may let the exam get the better of them; other test-takers may be unprepared—but not you. You will have taken all the steps you need to pass the U.S. Citizenship Exam.

Here's how the LearningExpress Test Preparation System works: The following easy steps lead you through everything you need to know and do to get ready to master your exam. Each of the steps listed below includes both reading about the step and one or more activities. It's important that you do the activities along with the reading, or you won't be getting the full benefit of the system. Each step tells you approximately how much time that step will take you to complete.

Step 1: Get Information	(30 minutes)
Step 2: Conquer Test Anxiety	(20 minutes)
Step 3: Make a Plan	(50 minutes)
Step 4: Reach Your Peak Performance Zone	(10 minutes)
Step 5: Get Your Act Together	(10 minutes)
Step 6: Do It!	(10 minutes)
Total time for complete system:	(130 minutes— 2 hours, 10 minutes)

We estimate that working through the entire system will take you less than two and a half hours, although it's perfectly OK if you work faster or slower. If you can take a whole afternoon or evening to prep, you can work through the whole LearningExpress Test Preparation System in one sitting. Otherwise, you can break it up, and do just one or two steps a day for the next several days. It's up to you—remember, you're in control.

Step 1: Get Information

Time to complete: 30 minutes
Activities: Read Introduction: How to Use this book
Knowledge is power. The first step in the Learning-Express Test Preparation System is finding out everything you can about the U.S. Citizenship Exam. Reading the first three chapters in this book will provide you with an overview of both the citizenship process and the exam. In addition, the U.S. Citizenship and Immigration Services division of the U.S. Department of Homeland Security has citizenship resources, including a guide to the exam and other material. The more details you can find out about the exam, the more efficiently you will be able to study.

What's on the U.S. Citizenship Exam

The U.S. Citizenship Exam tests you on U.S. government and history. It is administered in an interview format, during which the interviewer will ask you 10 questions from a set list of 100. You must answer 60% of the questions correctly. The interviewer will also ask you to write down one or two sentences that he or she will read.

Step 2: Conquer Test Anxiety

Time to complete: 20 minutes
Activity: Take the Test Stress Test
Having complete information about the test is the first step in getting control of the exam. Next, you have to overcome one of the biggest obstacles to test success: test anxiety. Test anxiety can not only impair your performance on the exam itself; it can even keep you from preparing properly. In this step, you will learn stress management techniques that will help you succeed on your exam. Learn these strategies now, and practice them as you work through the questions in this book, so they'll be second nature to you by exam day.

Combating Test Anxiety

The first thing you need to know is that a little test anxiety is a good thing. Everyone gets nervous before a big exam—and if that nervousness motivates you to prepare thoroughly, so much the better. In fact, it can even give you a little extra edge—just the kind of edge you need to do well on the exam.

On the following page is the Test Stress Test. Stop here and answer the questions on that page to find out whether your level of test anxiety is something you should worry about.

Stress Management before the Test

If you feel your level of anxiety getting the best of you in the weeks before the test, here is what you need to do to bring the level down again:

- **Get prepared.** There's nothing like knowing what to expect, and being prepared for it, to put you in control of test anxiety. That's why you're reading this book. Use it faithfully, and remind yourself that you're better prepared than most of the people taking the test.
- **Practice self-confidence.** A positive attitude is a great way to combat test anxiety. This is no time to be humble or shy. Stand in front of the mirror and say to your reflection, "I'm prepared. I'm full of self-confidence. I'm going to pass this exam. I know I can do it." Say it into a tape recorder and play it back once a day. If you hear it often enough, you will believe it.
- **Fight negative messages.** Every time someone starts telling you how hard the exam is, start telling them your self-confidence messages above. If the someone with the negative messages is you—telling yourself that you just can't do this—don't listen. Turn on your tape recorder and listen to your self-confidence messages.
- **Visualize.** Imagine the pride you will have when you become a U.S. citizen. Visualizing success can help make it happen—and it reminds you of why you're doing all this work in preparing for the exam.

- **Exercise.** Physical activity helps calm your body down and focus your mind. Besides, being in good physical shape can actually help you do well on the exam. Go for a run, lift weights, go swimming—and do it regularly.

Stress Management on Test Day

There are several ways you can bring down your level of test stress and anxiety on test day. They'll work best if you practice them in the weeks before the test, so you know which ones work best for you.

- **Deep breathing.** Take a deep breath while you count to five. Hold it for a count of one, and then let it out on a count of five. Repeat several times.
- **Move your body.** Try rolling your head in a circle. Rotate your shoulders. Shake your hands from the wrist. Many people find these movements very relaxing.
- **Visualize again.** Think of the place where you are most relaxed: lying on the beach in the sun, walking through the park, or whatever. Now, close your eyes and imagine you're actually there. If you practice in advance, you will find that you only need a few seconds of this exercise to experience a significant increase in your sense of well-being.

When anxiety threatens to overwhelm you *during the exam*, there are still things you can do to manage the stress level:

- **Repeat your self-confidence messages.** You should have them memorized by now. Say them quietly to yourself, and believe them!
- **Visualize one more time.** This time, visualize yourself answering the exam questions confidently and correctly. Like most visualization techniques, this one works best if you've practiced it ahead of time.

Try these techniques ahead of time, and see if they work for you!

You only need to worry about test anxiety if it is extreme enough to impair your performance. The following questionnaire will provide a diagnosis of your level of test anxiety. In the blank before each statement, write the number that most accurately describes your experience.

0 = Never
1 = Once or twice
2 = Sometimes
3 = Often

___ I have gotten so nervous before an exam that I simply put down the books and didn't study for it.

___ I have experienced disabling physical symptoms such as vomiting and severe headaches because I was nervous about an exam.

___ I have simply not showed up for an exam because I was scared to take it.

___ I have experienced dizziness and disorientation while taking an exam.

___ I have had trouble filling in the little circles because my hands were shaking too hard.

___ I have failed an exam because I was too nervous to complete it.

___ **Total: Add up the numbers in the blanks above.**

Your Test Stress Scores

Here are the steps you should take to combat test stress, depending on your score.

- **Below 3**: Your level of test anxiety is nothing to worry about; It's probably just enough to give you that little extra edge.

- **Between 3 and 6**: Your test anxiety may be enough to impair your performance, and you should practice the stress management techniques listed in this section to try to bring your test anxiety down to manageable levels.

- **Above 6**: Your level of test anxiety is a serious concern. In addition to practicing the stress management techniques listed in this section, you may want to seek additional help. Call your local high school or community college and ask for the academic counselor. Tell the counselor that you have a level of test anxiety that sometimes keeps you from being able to take the exam. The counselor may be willing to help you or may suggest someone else you should talk to.

Step 3: Make a Plan

Time to complete: 50 minutes
Activity: Construct a study plan

Maybe the most important thing you can do to get control of yourself and your exam is to make a study plan. Too many people fail to prepare simply because they fail to plan. Spending hours on the day before the exam poring over the 100 questions not only raises your level of test anxiety, it is simply no substitute for careful preparation and practice over time.

Don't fall into the cram trap. Take control of your preparation time by mapping out a study schedule. Depending on the amount of time you have before the exam, determine how much time you will devote to studying each week or, preferably, each day. If you're the kind of person who needs deadlines and assignments to motivate you for a project, lay them out in calendar form.

Even more important than making a plan is making a commitment. You can't learn U.S. civics and history overnight. You have to set aside some time every day for study and practice. Try for at least 20 minutes a day. Twenty minutes daily will do you much more good than two hours crammed into a Saturday.

If you have months before the exam, you're lucky. Don't put off your study until the week before the exam! Start now. Even ten minutes a day, with half an hour or more on weekends, can make a big difference in your performance.

Step 4: Reach Your Peak Performance Zone

Time to complete: 10 minutes to read; weeks to complete!
Activity: Complete the Physical Preparation Checklist

To get ready for a challenge like the U.S. Citizenship Exam, you have to take control of your physical, as well as your mental, state. Exercise, proper diet, and rest will ensure that your body works with, rather than against, your mind on test day, as well as during your preparation.

Exercise

If you don't already have a regular exercise program going, the time during which you're preparing for an exam is actually an excellent time to start one. And if you're already keeping fit—or trying to get that way—don't let the pressure of preparing for an exam fool you into quitting now. Exercise helps reduce stress by pumping wonderful good-feeling hormones called endorphins into your system. It also increases the oxygen supply throughout your body, including your brain, so you will be at peak performance on test day.

A half hour of vigorous activity—enough to raise a sweat—every day should be your aim. If you're really pressed for time, every other day is OK. Choose an activity you like and get out there and do it. Jogging with a friend always makes the time go faster, or take a radio.

But don't overdo it. You don't want to exhaust yourself. Moderation is the key.

Diet

First of all, cut out the junk. Go easy on caffeine and nicotine, and eliminate alcohol and any other drugs from your system at least two weeks before the exam.

What your body needs for peak performance is simply a balanced diet. Eat plenty of fruits and vegetables, along with protein and carbohydrates. Foods that are high in lecithin (an amino acid), such as fish and beans, are especially good brain foods.

The night before the exam, you might carbo-load the way athletes do before a contest. Eat a big plate of spaghetti, rice and beans, or whatever your favorite carbohydrate is.

Rest

You probably know how much sleep you need every night to be at your best, even if you don't always get it. Make sure you do get that much sleep, though, for at least a week before the exam. Moderation is important here, too. Too much sleep will just make you groggy.

If you're not a morning person and your exam appointment is in the morning, you should reset your internal clock so that your body doesn't think you're taking an exam at 3 A.M. You have to start this process well before the exam. The way it works is to get up half an hour earlier each morning, and then go to bed half an hour earlier that night. Don't try it the other way around; you will just toss and turn if you go to bed early without having gotten up early. The next morning, get up another half an hour earlier, and so on. How long you will have to do this depends on how late you're used to getting up. Use the Physical Preparation Checklist on the following page to make sure you're in tip-top form.

Step 5: Get Your Act Together

Time to complete: 10 minutes to read; time to complete will vary

Activity: Complete Final Preparations worksheet

You're in control of your mind and body; you're in charge of test anxiety, your preparation, and your test-taking strategies. Now, it's time to take charge of external factors, like the testing site and the materials you need to take the exam.

Find Out Where the Exam Is and Make a Trial Run

The USCIS will notify you when and where your exam is being held. Do you know how to get to the location? Do you know how long it will take to get there? If not, make a trial run, preferably on the same day of the week at the same time of day. Make note on the Final Preparations worksheet on page 26, of the amount of time it will take you to get to the exam site. Plan on arriving 10–15 minutes early so you can get the lay of the land,

use the bathroom, and calm down. Then figure out how early you will have to get up that morning, and make sure you get up that early every day for a week before the exam.

Gather Your Materials

The night before the exam, lay out the clothes you will wear and the materials you have to bring with you to the exam. Plan on dressing in layers; you won't have any control over the temperature of the examination room. Have a sweater or jacket you can take off if it's warm. Use the checklist on the Final Preparations worksheet to help you pull together what you will need

Don't Skip Breakfast

Even if you don't usually eat breakfast, do so on exam morning. A cup of coffee doesn't count. Don't do doughnuts or other sweet foods, either. A sugar high will leave you with a sugar low in the middle of the exam. A mix of protein and carbohydrates is best: cereal with milk and just a little sugar, or eggs with toast, will do your body a world of good.

Step 6: Do It!

Time to complete: 10 minutes, plus test-taking time
Activity: Pass the U.S. Citizenship Exam!

Fast forward to exam day. You're ready. You made a study plan and followed through. You practiced your test-taking strategies while working through this book. You're in control of your physical, mental, and emotional state. You know when and where to show up and what to bring with you. In other words, you're prepared for the exam.

Now you can go into the exam, full of confidence, armed with test-taking strategies you've practiced until they're second nature. You're in control of yourself, your environment, and your performance on the exam. You're ready to succeed. So do it. Go in there and pass the exam. And look forward to your future as a U.S. citizen!

For the week before the test, write down 1) what physical exercise you engaged in and for how long and 2) what you ate for each meal. Remember, you're trying for at least half an hour of exercise every other day (preferably every day) and a balanced diet that's light on junk food.

Exam minus 7 days

Exercise: _____ for _____ minutes

Breakfast:_____

Lunch:_____

Dinner:_____

Snacks:_____

Exam minus 6 days

Exercise: _____ for _____ minutes

Breakfast:_____

Lunch:_____

Dinner:_____

Snacks:_____

Exam minus 5 days

Exercise: _____ for _____ minutes

Breakfast:_____

Lunch:_____

Dinner:_____

Snacks:_____

Exam minus 4 days

Exercise: _____ for _____ minutes

Breakfast:_____

Lunch:_____

Dinner:_____

Snacks:_____

Exam minus 3 days

Exercise: _____ for _____ minutes

Breakfast:_____

Lunch:_____

Dinner:_____

Snacks:_____

Exam minus 2 days

Exercise: _____ for _____ minutes

Breakfast:_____

Lunch:_____

Dinner:_____

Snacks:_____

Exam minus 1 day

Exercise: _____ for _____ minutes

Breakfast:_____

Lunch:_____

Dinner:_____

Snacks:_____

Getting to the Exam Site

Location of exam site: _____

Date: _____

Departure time: _____

Do I know how to get to the exam site?   Yes ____   No ____

(If no, make a trial run.)

Time it will take to get to exam site: _____

Things to Lay Out the Night Before

Clothes I will wear   ____

Sweater/jacket   ____

Watch   ____

Photo ID   ____

Other Things to Bring/Remember

_____

_____

_____

_____

CHAPTER

5 ▶ AMERICA TODAY

In this chapter, we look at some of the important people and aspects of government in America today. We also review the symbols of America—the U.S. flag and the national anthem. We start by covering a few questions about citizenship and voting.

CITIZENSHIP AND VOTING

There are different paths to citizenship in the United States. Most Americans have been citizens for their entire lives, because they were born in America. People who love America but were not born here can also become citizens through the process of **naturalization**. Immigrants to the United States may apply to become American citizens after living in the United States as a **permanent resident** for five years. Immigrants that are married to U.S. citizens may apply for citizenship after being a permanent resident for three years.

Both **natural-born citizens** and **naturalized citizens** have all the rights and benefits that come with citizenship. The benefits to becoming a U.S. citizen include the right to vote, the right to travel with a U.S. passport, the right to serve on a jury, and the right to apply for federal jobs and to petition for close relatives to come to the United States to live. Voting and serving on a jury are important responsibilities of American citizens, and they are two rights that only citizens have. In addition to voting and serving on juries, American citizens have other important responsibilities, such as paying federal income taxes by **April 15** and registering for the **Selective Service**, which all males over 18 must do.

However, the most important right granted to U.S. citizens is the **right to vote**. This right is guaranteed to all citizens over the age of 18 by the Constitution, in amendments 14, 15, 19, 24, and 26. Starting from the **minimum voting age** of 18, American citizens can help choose which candidates will take office in government. The elections usually have candidates from the two major parties in the United States: the **Democratic Party** and the **Republican Party. The people** directly elect Congress through this voting process. The process is more indirect in presidential elections, where each state has a certain number of votes for the **Electoral College**, which is the group that actually elects the president. We vote for the president in November, and the new president is inaugurated, or sworn into office, in January.

Vote in November

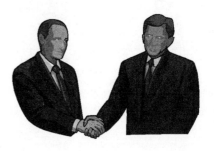

President inaugurated in January

Words to Know

Permanent resident: a noncitizen who lives legally in the United States

Naturalization: the process of becoming a citizen

Natural-born citizen: citizen by birth in the United States

Naturalized citizen: citizen who passed the citizenship test

Right to vote: most important right of U.S. citizens

Minimum voting age: youngest age at which a citizen can vote (18 in the United States)

Democratic Party/Democrat: one of the two major political parties in the United States/one who belongs to the Democratic Party

Republican Party/Republican: one of the two major political parties in the United States/one who belongs to the Republican Party

Electoral College: group that actually elects the president

The people: directly elect members of Congress

Related Questions

1. Q: Name one benefit of being a citizen.
A: One benefit is the ability . . . (choose one from below)
- **to obtain federal government jobs**
- **to travel with a U.S. passport**
- **to petition for close relatives to come to the United States to live**
- **to serve on a jury**
- **to vote**

2. Q: Name one important responsibility that is reserved especially for citizens.
A: Citizens can **vote** and **serve on a jury**.

3. Q: What is the minimum voting age in the United States?
A: The minimum voting age in the United States is **18**.

4. Q: What are you promising to do when you become a citizen?
A: You are promising to **give up loyalty to other countries**, **defend the Constitution** and **laws of the United States,** and **be loyal to the United States**.

5. Q: Who elects Congress?
A: **The people** elect Congress directly.

6. Q: Who elects the president of the United States?
A: **The Electoral College** elects the president of the United States.

7. Q: What are the two major political parties in the United States?
A: The two major political parties are **the Democratic** and **Republican parties**.

8. Q: When are your federal income taxes due?
A: Federal income taxes are due on **April 15**.

9. Q: When must all men register for the Selective Service?
A: All men must register for the Selective Service at **age 18**.

10. Q: Describe one amendment to the Constitution that deals with who can vote.
A: You can vote if you are **over age 18**. **People of any race and gender can vote**.

Exercises

Fill in the Blank
The answers to these five questions can be found on page 110.

1. The president of the United States is elected by the _____.

2. You must be at least _____ years old to vote in the United States.

3. The two major political parties in America are the _____ and the_____ parties.

4. The right to _____ is the most important right granted to American citizens.

5. Congress is directly _____ by the people.

Sentence Composition
Make up your own sentence using the words or phrases given.

1. _____

    (the people)

2. _____

    (citizenship)

3. _____

    (the right to vote)

4. _____

    (responsibility)

Multiple Choice

Choose the best answer for each question. Answers can be found on page 110.

1. Men must register for the Selective Service at age
   a. 21
   b. 30
   c. 18
   d. 16

2. A noncitizen who lives legally in the United States is called a
   a. permanent resident
   b. visiting resident
   c. sub-citizen
   d. permanent visitor

3. Which of the following is **not** a benefit solely of being a citizen?
   a. being able to vote
   b. being able to serve on a jury
   c. being able to obtain a drivers license
   d. being able to travel with the U.S. passport

Dictation Practice

Write each sentence twice. For the first time, you can look at the sentence. For the second time, try writing the sentence without looking.

1. I want to be a citizen.

2. I love America.

3. I want to be a citizen, because I love America.

4. I want to be an American.

5. Citizens have the right to vote.

1. _____

    _____

2. _____

    _____

3. _____

    _____

4. _____

    _____

5. _____

    _____

SYMBOLS OF AMERICA

Perhaps the most visible symbol of America is the **red**, **white**, and **blue American flag**. The **13 red** and **white stripes** represent the original 13 states, which were called **colonies**. The **50 white stars** signify the 50 states in the union now. However, besides representing America's past and present, the flag is also a symbol of freedom and the American spirit.

For example, our **national anthem**, called **"The Star-Spangled Banner,"** salutes the flag. It was written during the War of 1812. The anthem describes how the waving flag provided hope during an important battle, because it represents America—"the land of the free and the home of the brave."

The **Pledge of Allegiance** also declares loyalty to the American flag and the country it represents. Another important symbol of America is the **Statue of Liberty**. The Statue of Liberty was a gift from France in 1886. The statue is of a woman holding a torch in one hand and a book in the other, and it stands on Liberty Island, near New York's Ellis Island in New York Harbor. It has welcomed the many immigrants who entered the United States at Ellis Island, as the first visible symbol of the hope and freedom that America promises.

The Statue of Liberty

The American flag

The Pledge of Allegiance
I pledge allegiance, to the flag
of the United States of America.
And to the republic, for which it stands
One nation, under God, indivisible
With liberty and justice for all.

The Star-Spangled Banner
O say, can you see, by the Dawn's early light?
What so proudly we hailed at the twilight's last gleaming?
Whose broad stripes and bright stars, through the perilous fight,
O'er the ramparts we watched, were so gallantly streaming?
And the rockets' red glare, the bombs bursting in air,
Gave proof through the night that our flag was still there
O say, does that star-spangled banner yet wave
O'er the land of the free and the home of the brave?

Words to Know

American flag: a symbol of America that is red, white, and blue
Red, white, and blue: the colors of the flag
Stars: 50 stars on the American flag, representing the number of states in the Union
Stripes: 13 stripes on the American flag, representing the original states
National anthem: the country's official song
"The Star-Spangled Banner": American national anthem
Colonies: original 13 states in America

Related Questions

1. Q: What are the colors of the American flag?
A: The colors of the American flag are **red**, **white**, and **blue**.

2. Q: Why are there 50 stars on the flag?
A: There are 50 stars on the flag because **there are 50 states**, and each star represents one state.

3. Q: Why are there 13 stripes on the flag?
A: There are 13 stripes on the flag because **there were 13 original colonies**, and each stripe represents one original colony.

4. Q: Who do we show loyalty to when we say the Pledge of Allegiance?
A: We show loyalty to **the United States**, or **the flag of the United States**.

5. Q: Where is the Statue of Liberty located?
A: The Statue of Liberty is located on Liberty Island, near **Ellis Island**.

6. Q: What is the national anthem of the United States?
A: The national anthem of the United States is **"The Star-Spangled Banner."**

7. Q: How many states are there in the union?
A: There are **50** states in the union.

8. Q: Name the 13 original colonies.
A: The colonies were Connecticut, Delaware, Georgia, Maryland, Massachusetts, New Hampshire, New Jersey, New York, North Carolina, Pennsylvania, Rhode Island, South Carolina, and Virginia.

Exercises

Fill in the Blank

The answers to these four questions can be found on page 110.

1. The colors of the flag are _____, _____, and _____.

2. The stars on the flag represent _____.

3. The _____ on the flag represent the 13 original colonies.

4. Our national anthem is called _____.

Sentence Composition

Make up your own sentence using the words or phrases given.

1. _____

    (the American flag)

2. _____

    (13 original states)

3. _____

    ("The Star-Spangled Banner")

Multiple Choice

Choose the best answer for each question. Answers can be found on page 110.

1. The United States has how many states?
    a. 13
    b. 50
    c. 26
    d. 48

2. Which of the following was **not** one of the original 13 colonies?
    a. New Hampshire
    b. New York
    c. Virginia
    d. Main

3. "The Star-Spangled Banner" is the
    a. American hymn
    b. National anthem
    c. Pledge of allegiance
    d. Anthem of peace

Dictation Practice

Write each sentence twice. For the first time, you can look at the sentence. For the second time, try writing the sentence without looking.

1. America is the home of the brave.

2. America is the land of the free.

3. The Statue of Liberty was a gift from France.

4. I pledge allegiance to the flag of the United States of America.

5. There are 13 Stripes on the American flag.

1. _____

   _____

2. _____

   _____

3. _____

   _____

4. _____

   _____

5. _____

   _____

AMERICA AROUND YOU

Abraham Lincoln called the American system of government a "government of the people, by the people, and for the people." While the people do not all directly make decisions in government, American citizens do choose their leaders by voting for candidates, who usually come from the two major political parties: the Democrats and the Republicans. This system of representative government is called a **democratic republic**. The government is based in the capital of the United States, **Washington, D.C.**

In the American system of government, power is divided up by checks and balances between the three **branches** of government: **legislative**, **executive**, and **judicial**. The legislative branch makes laws, the executive branch enforces the laws, and the judicial branch interprets the laws through the court system. At the federal level, the legislative branch is Congress, the executive branch is the president and the cabinet, and the judicial branch is the Supreme Court. The system of **checks and balances** prevents any one branch of government from becoming too powerful. You will learn more about the three branches of government in Chapter 6.

You may have heard of **President Barack Obama**, **Vice President Joe Biden**, and **Supreme Court Chief Justice John Roberts**. (Note: These names and titles were accurate at the time this book was published.) However, your state and local officials serve important roles as well. A governor is in charge of running the government of a state, while a mayor is in charge of running the government of a city. Who are your governor and mayor? Do you know your state's senators? What about your local officials?

In addition to the system of government, the economic system is an important aspect of the country that you live in. The United States has a **capitalist economy** that is based on **free markets**.

Three branches of government

Words to Know

Democratic republic: system of government in which citizens elect representatives to govern

Washington, D.C.: the capital of the United States

Branch: part

Legislative: branch of government that makes federal laws

Executive: branch of government that enforces laws

Judicial: branch of government that interprets the laws

President: chief executive of the federal government

Governor: head executive of a state

Mayor: head executive of a city

Checks and balances: system that prevents one branch of the government from becoming too powerful

Capitalist economy: economic system that the United States uses; based on free markets

Related Questions

1. Q: What kind of government does the United States have?

A: The U.S. government is a **democratic republic**.

2. Q: How many branches are there in our government?

A: There are **three** branches.

3. Q: What are the three branches of our government?

A: The three branches of government are the **legislative**, **executive**, and **judicial**.

4. Q: Who are the two senators from your state?

A: My senators are _____ and _____. (Look up your state's senators.)

5. Q: What is the capital of your state?

A: My state's capital is _____. (Look up your state's capital.)

6. Q: Who is the governor of your state?

A: My governor is _____. (Look up your state's governor.)

7. Q: Who is the head of your local government?

A: The head of my local government is _____. (Look up your city's head executive.)

8. Q: What stops one branch of government from becoming too powerful?

A: **The system of checks and balances** prevents one branch of government from becoming too powerful.

9. Q: Who is your U.S. representative?

A: My U.S. representative is _____. (Look up your U.S. representative.)

10. Q: What kind of economic system do we have in the United States?

A: We have a **capitalist economy** in the United States.

Bonus Review

1. Q: How many states are there in the union?

A: There are _____ states in the union.

2. Q: What are the two major political parties in the United States?

A: The two major political parties in the United States are the _____ and the _____.

Exercises

Fill in the Blank

The answers to these five questions can be found on page 110.

1. The head executive of a state is a _____.

2. The _____ branch of government makes the federal laws.

3. _____ is the capital of the United States of America.

4. The system of government of the United States in which citizens elect representatives to govern them is a _____.

5. The _____, the vice president, and the _____ make up the executive branch.

Sentence Composition

Make up your own sentence using the words or phrases given.

1. _____

    (judicial branch)

2. _____

    (governor)

3. _____

    (Washington, D.C.)

Multiple Choice

Choose the best answer for each question. Answers can be found on page 110.

1.   Which of the following is **not** one of the three branches of government?
     a. legislative
     b. executive
     c. economic
     d. judicial

2.   A governor is the
     a. head executive of a city.
     b. leader of congress.
     c. head executive of state.
     d. head executive of a county.

3.   How many senators does each state have?
     a. A number that varies depending on population
     b. 1
     c. 5
     d. 2

Dictation Practice

Write each sentence twice. For the first time, you can look at the sentence. For the second time, try writing the sentence without looking.

1. The U.S. government is divided into three branches.

2. Congress meets in Washington, D.C.

3. The president enforces the laws.

4. A governor is the head executive of a state.

5. The judicial branch interprets the laws.

1. _____

_____

2. _____

_____

3. _____

_____

4. _____

_____

5. _____

_____

4 ▶ AMERICAN GEOGRAPHY

The United States is a large country with an interesting geography. With a land mass of 9.8 million square kilometers, the United States is the second largest country in North America. Canada is the largest country with a land mass of 9.9 million square kilometers. The United States borders **Canada** to the north and **Mexico** to the south. Some of the states that border Canada are **Maine**, **New York**, **Minnesota**, **North Dakota**, **Montana**, and **Washington**. The states that have borders with Mexico are **Texas**, **New Mexico**, **Arizona**, and **California**. The country has large oceans on either side of it. The **Atlantic Ocean** lies on the east coast of the United States, and the **Pacific Ocean** lies on the west coast.

The country is made up of 50 states, **Washington, D.C.**, and five territories. The capital of the United States is Washington, D.C. Every state has a capital as well. Do you know the capital of your state? The U.S. territories are **Puerto Rico**, **Guam**, **the U.S. Virgin Islands**, **the Northern Mariana Islands**, and **American Samoa**.

Because the United States is so big, its land has many interesting features, including rivers and mountains. The longest rivers in the country are the **Mississippi** and the **Missouri**, which run through the center of the country. The highest mountain is **Mt. McKinley**, or **Denali**, which is located in Alaska.

Words to Know

Atlantic Ocean: ocean on the east coast of the United States
Pacific Ocean: ocean on the west coast of the United States
Mississippi River: longest river in the United States
Washington, D.C.: capital of the United States
Canada: the country to the north of the United States
Mexico: the country to the south of the United States

Related Questions

1. Q: On what continent is the United States located?
A: The United States is located on **North America**.

2. Q: What ocean is on the east coast of the United States?
A: The **Atlantic Ocean** is on the east coast of the United States.

3. Q: What ocean is on the west coast of the United States?
A: The **Pacific Ocean** is on the west coast of the United States.

4. Q: Name one U.S. territory.
A: U.S. territories include **Puerto Rico, Guam, U.S. Virgin Islands, Northern Mariana Islands**, and **American Samoa**.

5. Q: What is the tallest mountain in the United States?
A: The tallest mountain in the United States is **Mt. McKinley (Denali)**.

6. Q: What are the longest rivers in the United States?
A: The longest rivers in the United States are the **Mississippi River** and the **Missouri River**.

7. Q: Name one state that borders Canada.
A: The states that border Canada include **Maine, New York, Minnesota, North Dakota, Montana**, and **Washington**.

8. Q: Name one state that borders Mexico.
A: The states that border Mexico include **California, New Mexico, Arizona**, and **Texas**.

9. Q: What is the capital of the United States?
A: The capital of the United States is **Washington, D.C.**

Exercises

Fill in the Blank
The answers to these five questions can be found on page 111.

1. The United States is bordered by _____ to the north and _____ to the south.

2. Guam and Puerto Rico are examples of United States _____.

3. The Mississippi and the Missouri are the country's two longest _____.

4. Minnesota is a state that borders _____.

5. California is a state that borders _____.

Sentence Composition
Make up your own sentence using the words or phrases given.

1. _____
   (rivers)

2. _____
   (capital)

3. _____
   (ocean)

Multiple Choice

Choose the best answer for each question. Answers can be found on page 111.

1. How many territories does the United States have?
   a. 50
   b. 5
   c. none
   d. 13

2. What is the capital of the United States?
   a. Texas
   b. New York
   c. Washington, D.C.
   d. Liberty Island

3. Guam is
   a. the 50th U.S. state.
   b. A U.S. territory.
   c. the country that borders California to the south.
   d. the capital of Florida.

Dictation Practice

Write each sentence twice. For the first time, you can look at the sentence. For the second time, try writing the sentence without looking.

1.   The United States is the second-largest country in North America.

2.   I like to live in America.

3.   She lives in California.

4.   Texas borders Mexico.

5.   The United States has five territories.

1.   _____

_____

2.   _____

_____

3.   _____

_____

4.   _____

_____

5.   _____

_____

5 ▶ AMERICAN HOLIDAYS

American people celebrate several important national **holidays** that occur throughout the year. Perhaps the most important holiday is **Independence Day**, which we celebrate on July 4 to celebrate the country's independence from Great Britain. Other important holidays are **Veterans Day** and **Memorial Day**, which celebrate people who have fought for the country in wars; **Thanksgiving**, a celebration of the pilgrims' friendship with the Native Americans; **Presidents Day**, also celebrated as Washington's birthday; and **Martin Luther King, Jr., Day**, which honors an important American who you will read about soon.

Words to Know

Holiday: a special day of celebration for everyone in the country
Independence Day: the celebration of America's independence from Great Britain, celebrated on July 4

Related Questions

1. **Q:** When do we celebrate Independence Day?
A: We celebrate Independence Day on **July 4**.

2. **Q:** Can you name some other national holidays that Americans celebrate?
A: Some other holidays include **Thanksgiving**, **Memorial Day**, **Veterans Day**, and **Martin Luther King, Jr., Day**.

Exercises

Fill in the Blank

The answers to these questions can be found on page 111.

1. The important holiday on July 4 is _____.

2. Thanksgiving, Veterans Day, and Memorial Day are all examples of _____.

Sentence Composition

Make up your own sentence using the words or phrases given.

1. _____

(Thanksgiving)

2. _____

(holiday)

Dictation Practice

Write each sentence twice. For the first time, you can look at the sentence. For the second time, try writing the sentence without looking.

1. I like to celebrate on holidays.

2. Independence Day is a very important holiday.

3. Martin Luther King, Jr., Day is an American holiday.

4. Thanksgiving is celebrated in November.

1. _____

_____

2. _____

_____

3. _____

_____

4. _____

_____

CHAPTER

6

AMERICAN HISTORY

This chapter will teach you some basics about United States history. It starts with the birth of the United States and covers the major wars and movements, from the American Revolution to the civil rights movement.

Lesson 8:   The Civil War and Modern History   71

Key Concepts:

- The Civil War
- Abraham Lincoln and the Emancipation Proclamation
- World War I and World War II
- Alaska and Hawaii
- Dr. Martin Luther King, Jr., and the civil rights movement

6 ▶ THE 13 COLONIES

The history of the United States government begins with the **13 original states**, which were called **colonies**. These states were settled by groups of colonists who came to America from Great Britain. The **pilgrims** were the first of these American colonists, and they came to America for **religious freedom**. When they arrived in America, the winters were very hard. It was only with the help of the **Native Americans (or American Indians)** that the pilgrims survived. To give thanks for their help and for their new homes, the colonists celebrated **Thanksgiving** with the Native Americans. Some of the Native American tribes are named the **Cherokee**, **Navajo**, **Sioux**, **Apache**, and **Creek**, but there are many more as well.

In all, there were **13 colonies: Connecticut**, **Delaware**, **Georgia**, **Maryland**, **Massachusetts**, **New Hampshire**, **New Jersey**, **New York**, **North Carolina**, **Pennsylvania**, **Rhode Island**, **South Carolina**, and **Virginia**. The king of Great Britain, King George III, ruled the colonies.

The 13 colonies

Words to Know

Colonies: the 13 original states
Pilgrims: the first American colonists
Religious freedom: being allowed to practice any religion
Native Americans (American Indians): people who lived in America before the pilgrims arrived
Thanksgiving: holiday celebrated for the first time by the American colonists to thank the Native Americans

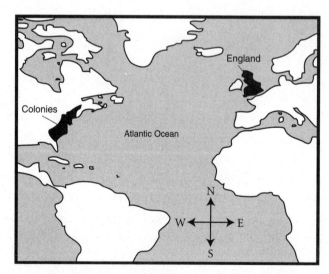

The colonies sought freedom from England

Related Questions

1. Q: Why did the pilgrims come to America?
A: The pilgrims came to America for **religious freedom**.

2. Q: Who lived in America before the pilgrims arrived?
A: The Native Americans, or **American Indians**, lived in America before the pilgrims arrived.

3. Q: Name a Native American tribe.
A: The Native American tribes include the **Cherokee**, **Navajo**, **Sioux**, **Apache**, and **Creek**.

4. Q: What holiday was celebrated for the first time by the American colonists?
A: Thanksgiving was celebrated for the first time by the American colonists.

5. Q: What were the 13 original states called?
A: The 13 original states were called **the 13 colonies**.

6. Q: Can you name the 13 original states?
A: The 13 original states were **Connecticut**, **Delaware**, **Georgia**, **Maryland**, **Massachusetts**, **New Hampshire**, **New Jersey**, **New York**, **North Carolina**, **Pennsylvania**, **Rhode Island**, **South Carolina**, and **Virginia**

Pilgrims

Exercises

Fill in the Blank
The answers to these five questions can be found on page 111.

1. The _____ were the first American colonists.

2. The 13 original states were called _____.

3. The _____ lived in America before the colonists arrived.

4. _____ is the holiday that was first celebrated by the American colonists.

5. The pilgrims came to America for _____.

Sentence Composition
Make up your own sentence using the words or phrases given.

1. _____
    (Native Americans)

2. _____
    (pilgrims)

3. _____
    (13 colonies)

Dictation Practice

Write each sentence twice. For the first time, you can look at the sentence. For the second time, try writing the sentence without looking.

1. The American flag has 13 stripes.

2. She speaks English very well.

3. They buy many things at the store.

4. Rhode Island was one of the 13 colonies.

5. Thanksgiving is a holiday.

1. _____

   _____

2. _____

   _____

3. _____

   _____

4. _____

   _____

5. _____

   _____

THE AMERICAN REVOLUTION

The colonies did not like being ruled by King George III, because they had no say in government but still had to pay taxes to Great Britain. So the American colonists decided to fight for their freedom from Great Britain.

On July 4, 1776, the American colonies adopted the **Declaration of Independence**, which **Thomas Jefferson** and others had written. The basic beliefs of the Declaration are that **all men are created equal** and that all people have the right to life, liberty, and the pursuit of happiness. This started the **Revolutionary War**, also known as the **American Revolution**. In the United States, **Independence Day** is a federal holiday celebrated every **July 4**, signifying the United States' declaration of independence from the kingdom of Great Britain.

George Washington was the first **commander in chief** of the new country's army. Under Washington's leadership, the U.S. army defeated the English in 1783. George Washington was unanimously elected the first president of the United States. For his important role in American history, George Washington is known as the **"father of our country."**

After the United States achieved independence, its leaders met in 1787 to write a **Constitution** (this is discussed more in Lesson 9). This was called the **Constitutional Convention**. One important member of this convention was **Benjamin Franklin**. He was the oldest member of the convention, a U.S. diplomat, the first postmaster general of the United States, and the author of *Poor Richard's Almanac*. Before the Constitution was ratified, the **Federalist Papers** explained the purpose and meaning of the proposed Constitution, and promoted ratification. They were written by **James Madison**, **Alexander Hamilton**, and **John Jay**, but were published under the pseudonym, or fictitious name, **"Publius."**

Thomas Jefferson

Words to Know

Declaration of Independence: document written in 1776 declaring independence from Great Britain

Thomas Jefferson: main writer of the Declaration of Independence

All men are created equal: basic belief of the Declaration of Independence

Revolutionary War, or American Revolution: war to fight for freedom from Great Britain

Independence Day: a federal holiday celebrated July 4; celebrates the declaration of independence from Great Britain

George Washington: first commander in chief and president, father of our country

Benjamin Franklin: oldest delegate at the Constitutional Convention; he was also a diplomat, the postmaster general, and the author of *Poor Richard's Almanac*

Federalist Papers: documents that supported the passage of the Constitution, written by Alexander Hamilton, James Madison, and John Jay (Publius)

Signing the Declaration of Independence

Relevant Questions

1. Q: What country did America fight during the Revolutionary War?
A: America fought **Great Britain** during the Revolutionary War.

2. Q: What did the Declaration of Independence do?
A: The **Declaration of Independence announced our independence from Great Britain.**

3. Q: What is the date of Independence Day?
A: Independence Day is on **July 4.**

4. Q: Independence Day celebrates independence from whom?
A: Independence Day celebrates independence from **Great Britain.**

5. Q: When was the Declaration of Independence adopted?
A: The Declaration of Independence was adopted on **July 4, 1776.**

6. Q: The Declaration of Independence lists rights that all people have. What are two of these rights?
A: These rights include **life**, **liberty**, and **the pursuit of happiness.**

7. Q: Who was the main writer of the Declaration of Independence?
A: **Thomas Jefferson** was the main writer of the Declaration of Independence.

8. Q: Who was the first president of the United States?
A: **George Washington** was the first president of the United States.

9. Q: Which president is called the "father of our country"?
A: **George Washington** is called the "father of our country."

10. Q: Which president was the first commander in chief of the U.S. Army?
A: **George Washington** was the first commander in chief of the U.S. Army.

11. Q: What makes Benjamin Franklin famous?
A: Benjamin Franklin was **the oldest member of the Constitutional Convention, the first postmaster general of the United States, a U.S. diplomat,** and **the author of *Poor Richard's Almanac*.**

12. Q: Name one of the writers of the Federalist Papers.
A: The writers of the Federalist Papers included **Alexander Hamilton, James Madison,** and **John Jay (Publius).**

George Washington

Exercises

Fill in the Blank

The answers to these six questions can be found on page 111.

1. The Declaration of Independence was adopted on _____.

2. Alexander Hamilton and John Jay were two of the writers of _____.

3. The oldest member of the Constitutional Convention was _____.

4. The main writer of the Declaration of Independence was _____.

5. _____ was the first commander in chief of the U.S. Army.

6. One of the main beliefs of the _____ is that all men are created equal.

Sentence Composition

Make up your own sentence using the words or phrases given.

1. _____

(George Washington)

2. _____

(July 4, 1776)

3. _____

(independence)

Multiple Choice

Choose the best answer for each question. Answers can be found on page 111.

1. Which of the following statements about George Washington is **not** true?
   a. He is called the "father of our country."
   b. He was the first commander in chief of the U.S. Army
   c. He wrote the Federalist Papers.
   d. He was the first president of the United States.

2. What was the war to fight for freedom from Great Britain called?
   a. The Civil War
   b. The American Revolution
   c. The British War
   d. The Great War

3. When was the Constitutional Convention held?
   a. 1787
   b. 1776
   c. 1777
   d. 1783

Dictation Practice

Write each sentence twice. For the first time, you can look at the sentence. For the second time, try writing the sentence without looking.

1. George Washington is known as the "father of our country."

2. America is the land of freedom.

3. The Revolutionary War was fought against Great Britain.

1. _____

_____

2. _____

_____

3. _____

_____

8 ▶ THE CIVIL WAR AND MODERN HISTORY

After the Constitution was written, the country expanded in size. In 1803, the United States became much larger when it purchased **the Louisiana Territory** from France. As the country grew and added more states to the union, tensions grew between the states of the south, which owned slaves who had been sold to them from Africa, and the north, which had made **slavery** illegal. In 1861, some states of the south decided to **secede** and leave the union to start their own country. This caused the **Civil War**, which was fought from 1861–1865 between the northern and southern states. **Abraham Lincoln** was the president during the Civil War, and he wrote the **Emancipation Proclamation** to free the slaves. In 1865, the north, led by Lincoln, won the war and slavery was ended.

By the twentieth century, the United States had become a major force on the world stage. From 1917–1918, the United States fought in **World War I. Woodrow Wilson** was the president at this time. America's role in **World War II** established our country as a world leader. America and its allies fought against Germany, Italy, and Japan, and helped to win the war in 1945. **Franklin Delano Roosevelt (FDR)** was the president during this war. **Dwight Eisenhower**, who later became president, was a general during this war. From the 1950s–1990s, the United States participated in a **cold war** against the former Soviet Union, which was a struggle against **communism**; it also fought wars in Korea (**the Korean War**), Vietnam (**the Vietnam War**) and in the Persian Gulf (**the Persian Gulf War**).

In the 1960s, the **civil rights movement** fought for the rights of groups that had been treated unfairly. **Dr. Martin Luther King, Jr.**, fought for the equality of all Americans, and 100 years before him, **Susan B. Anthony** struggled for the rights of women.

On **September 11, 2001**, a great tragedy occurred when terrorists attacked the United States.

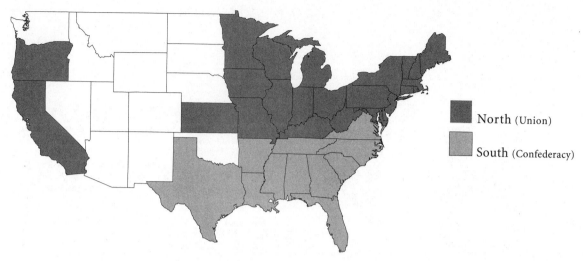

North (Union)

South (Confederacy)

The Civil War

Words to Know

Louisiana Territory: large territory the United States purchased from France in 1803

Slavery: the practice of owning other people

Secede: leave the union

Civil War: the war between the north and the south of America, from 1861–1865

Abraham Lincoln: the 16th president, who led the north to win the Civil War

Emancipation Proclamation: freed the slaves, written by Abraham Lincoln

Susan B. Anthony: a civil rights leader who fought for women's rights

Woodrow Wilson: U.S. president during World War I

World War II: a war in which America and its allies fought against Germany, Italy, and Japan

Franklin Delano Roosevelt (FDR): U.S. president during World War II

Dwight Eisenhower: general during World War II and later a president of the United States

Civil rights: equal rights for all citizens

Dr. Martin Luther King, Jr.: a civil rights leader

Persian Gulf War: a conflict to eject Iraqi forces from Kuwait in the 1990s

September 11, 2001: the date of a terrorist attack on the United States

Abraham Lincoln

Related Questions

1. Q: Name a war the United States fought during the 1800s.
   A: The United States fought the **Civil War** during the 1800s.

2. Q: What continent did the slaves come from?
   A: The slaves came from **Africa.**

3. Q: What is one important thing Abraham Lincoln did as president?
   A: Abraham Lincoln **led the United States during the Civil War, freed the slaves,** and **preserved the union.**

4. Q: What did the Emancipation Proclamation do?
   A: The Emancipation Proclamation **freed the slaves in the south.**

5. Q: What was the war that was fought between the northern and southern states?
   A: The **Civil War** was fought between the northern and southern states.

6. Q: Who was Susan B. Anthony and what did she do?
   A: Susan B. Anthony was **a civil rights leader who fought for women's rights.**

7. Q: What did Dr. Martin Luther King, Jr., do?
   A: Martin Luther King, Jr., **fought for equal rights for all Americans.**

8. Q: Who was our president during World War I?
   A: **Woodrow Wilson** was president during World War I.

9. Q: Before he was president, Eisenhower was a general. During what war was he a general?
   A: Eisenhower was a general during **World War II.**

10. Q: What was the United States fighting against during the Cold War?
   A: The United States fought against **communism** during the Cold War.

11. Q: What movement sought to end discrimination and provide rights for everyone?
   A: The **civil rights movement** sought to end discrimination and provide rights for everyone.

12. Q: What happened on September 11, 2001?
   A: **Terrorists attacked the United States** on September 11, 2001.

13. Q: What war was fought in the 1990s?
   A: The **Persian Gulf War** was fought in the 1990s.

Dr. Martin Luther King, Jr.

Exercises

Fill in the Blank

The answers to these seven questions can be found on page 112.

1. The United States purchased _____ from France in 1803.

2. In _____, the northern states of the United States fought against the southern states and won.

3. A primary reason for the Civil War was _____.

4. Abraham Lincoln's _____ freed the slaves.

5. The president of the United States during World War II was _____.

6. The _____ movement worked to end discrimination.

7. On September 11, 2001, _____ attacked the United States.

Multiple Choice

Choose the best answer for each question. Answers can be found on page 112.

1. Civil rights means
   a. that citizens must be polite to one another.
   b. equal rights for all citizens.
   c. the ability to leave the union.
   d. the right to bear arms.

2. Who was the president during World War I?
   a. Woodrow Wilson
   b. Thomas Jefferson
   c. James Madison
   d. Dwight Eisenhower

3. The Cold War describes a struggle between the U.S. and which other country?
   a. Italy
   b. Great Britain
   c. Soviet Union
   d. France

Sentence Composition

Make up your own sentence using the words or phrases given.

1. _____

   (civil rights)

2. _____

   (freedom)

3. _____

   (World War II)

Dictation Practice

Write each sentence twice. For the first time, you can look at the sentence. For the second time, try writing the sentence without looking.

1. Many people have died for freedom.

2. It is important for citizens to vote.

3. You work very hard at your job.

1. _____

   _____

2. _____

   _____

3. _____

   _____

C H A P T E R

THE U.S. GOVERNMENT

The U.S. government follows a system of checks and balances, with each of the three branches of government balancing the others. First, we will review the Constitution, which is the foundation of American government and laws. Next, we will examine each of the three branches of government.

Here is a chart to help you sort out the three branches of government at the various levels:

	Legislative		Executive	Judicial
Federal Government	**House of Representatives**	**Senate**	president, vice president, cabinet	Supreme Court (justices)
State Government	**State House of Representatives**	**State Senate**	governor	State Supreme Court
Municipal (City) Government	city council		mayor	municipal court

9 ▶ THE CONSTITUTION

The **Constitution** is the supreme law of the land. It was written in 1787, after the Americans won their freedom from Great Britain, in order to define the branches of government and establish a structure for the new nation of America. The **Preamble**, or introduction to the Constitution, begins with the words, "We the people of the United States."

The supreme law of the land also allows for changes to the Constitution itself, which are called **amendments**. Since 1787, 27 amendments to the Constitution have been passed. The first ten amendments are called the **Bill of Rights**. They were passed immediately to guarantee the rights and freedoms to all people in America. Some of these include **freedom of speech**, **freedom of press**, and **freedom of religion**.

The Constitution sets up the **rule of law**, the idea that no one is above the law and that leaders and the government must follow the same law as everyone else.

Furthermore, the Constitution sets up the structure of the government, dividing it into the **legislative branch**, the **executive branch**, and the **judicial branch**. It divides power between the **federal government**, or government at the national level, and state and local governments. The federal government has certain important powers, including the power to print money and to sign treaties. State and city governments have other jobs, including providing education and providing police and fire departments. It also lists the basic rights that everyone has.

The Constitution

Words to Know

Constitution: the supreme law of the land

Preamble: the introduction to the Constitution

Amendments: changes to the Constitution

Bill of Rights: the first ten amendments

Rule of law: the idea that the government must follow the law and that no one is above the law

Federal government: government at the national level, consisting of the legislative, executive, and judicial branches

Related Questions

1. Q: What does the Constitution do?

A: The Constitution **sets up the government, protects the basic rights of Americans,** and **establishes the rule of law.**

2. Q: What is the supreme law of the United States?

A: **The Constitution** is the supreme law of the United States.

3. Q: In what year was the Constitution written?

A: The Constitution was written in **1787.**

4. Q: What is the introduction to the Constitution called?

A: The introduction to the Constitution is called **the Preamble.**

5. Q: How does the Preamble to the Constitution begin?

A: The Preamble begins, **"We the people of the United States."**

6. Q: What is an amendment?

A: An amendment is a **change or addition to the Constitution.**

7. Q: How many amendments does the Constitution have?

A: The Constitution has **27 amendments.**

8. Q: What are first ten amendments called?

A: The first ten amendments are called the **Bill of Rights.**

9. Q: What does freedom of religion mean?

A: Freedom of religion means **the right to practice any religion or no religion at all.**

10. Q: Name three rights or freedoms guaranteed by the Bill of Rights.

A: Three rights or freedoms guaranteed by the Bill of Rights are **freedom of speech**, **freedom of press**, and **freedom of religion.**

11. Q: Whose rights are guaranteed by the Constitution and the Bill of Rights?

A: The rights of **all people in America** are guaranteed by the Constitution.

12. Q: What is the idea behind the rule of law?

A: The rule of law says that **no one is above the law and everyone must obey it.**

13. Q: Name the three branches of government.

A: The three branches of government are **legislative**, **executive**, and **judicial.**

14. Q: What is a power the federal government has under the Constitution?

A: The federal government can **print money**, **declare war**, **create an army**, and **make treaties.**

15. Q: What is one power of a state government?

A: The state government can **provide education**, **police and fire departments**, and **issue driver's licenses.**

Exercises

Fill in the Blank

The answers to these six questions can be found on page 112.

1.   The _____ is the supreme law of the land.

2.   The _____ is the introduction to the Constitution.

3.   There have been 27 _____ to the Constitution.

4.   The first ten amendments are called the _____.

5.   Freedom of _____ is guaranteed by one of the ten amendments.

6.   "_____" are the first three words of the Preamble.

Sentence Composition

Make up your own sentence using the words or phrases given.

1.   _____
     (rights)

2.   _____
     (Constitution)

3.   _____
     (freedom of speech)

The Bill of Rights

Dictation Practice

Write each sentence twice. For the first time, you can look at the sentence. For the second time, try writing the sentence without looking.

1. The Constitution is the supreme law of our land.

2. The people have a voice in government.

3. The people in the class took a citizenship test.

4. An amendment is a change to the Constitution.

5. The Bill of Rights guarantees the freedom of speech.

1. _____

    _____

2. _____

    _____

3. _____

_____

4. _____

_____

5. _____

_____

10 ▶ THE LEGISLATIVE BRANCH

The **legislative branch** of government makes the laws. At the federal level, the legislative branch is **Congress**, which makes the federal laws and also has the power to declare war. Congress is made up of the **Senate** and the **House of Representatives**, and its members are elected directly by the people. Both halves of Congress meet in the **U.S. Capitol** building in **Washington, D.C.**

The Capitol

The **Senate** is the smaller group, with 100 **senators**, two from each of the 50 states. Senators are elected for six-year **terms**. The vice president presides over the Senate. The larger **House of Representatives** has 435 **representatives**, who are elected for two-year terms. The number of representatives for each state is determined by the total population of each state and each state must have at least one representative. The Speaker of the House presides over the House of Representatives. There is no limit to the number of times a senator or representative may be reelected.

Senators

California

Rhode Island

Representatives

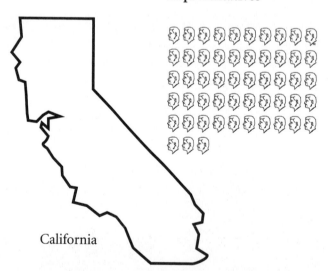

California

Rhode Island

Words to Know

Legislative branch: the branch of government that makes laws
Congress: the legislative branch of government at the federal level
Senate: one of the groups that make up Congress; has 100 members
House of Representatives: one of the groups that make up Congress; has 435 members
U.S. Capitol: a building in Washington, D.C., where Congress meets
Senator: a member of Senate
Term: period of time in office
Representative: a member of the House of Representatives

Related Questions

1. Q: At the federal level, what is the legislative branch of government?
A: The legislative branch at the federal level is **Congress.**

2. Q: Who makes the federal laws in the United States?
A: Congress makes the federal laws.

3. Q: What are the two parts of Congress?
A: The **Senate** and **the House of Representatives** are the two parts of Congress.

4. Q: What group has the power to declare war?
A: Congress has the power to declare war.

5. Q: Who elects members of Congress?
A: The people directly elect members of Congress.

6. Q: Who is one of your state's senators?
A: My state's senator is _____. (Look up your state's senators.)

7. Q: How many senators are there in Congress?
A: There are **100** senators in Congress.

8. Q: Who does a state senator represent in Congress?
A: The state senator **represents all the people of his or her state.**

9. Q: For how long do we elect each senator?
A: We elect senators for **six-year terms.**

10. **Q:** How many times may a senator or representative be reelected?

A: **There is no limit** to the number of times a senator or representative may be reelected.

11. **Q:** How many representatives are in the House of Representatives?

A: The House of Representatives has **435 representatives**.

12. **Q:** For how long do we elect representatives?

A: We elect representatives for **two-year terms**.

13. **Q:** Where does Congress meet?

A: Congress meets **in the U.S. Capitol building in Washington, D.C.**

14. **Q:** : Name your U.S. representative.

A: My U.S. representative is _____. (Look up your U.S. representative.)

15. **Q:** Why do some states have more U.S. representatives than others?

A: States that have **more people** have more representatives.

Exercises

Fill in the Blank

The answers to these six questions can be found on page 112.

1. Congress is made up of the _____ and the _____.

2. Only _____ has the power to declare war.

3. Congress meets in the U.S. _____ building.

4. We elect each _____ for two-year terms.

5. There is no limit to how many _____ a senator or representative may serve.

6. States with larger populations have _____ U.S. representatives.

Sentence Composition

Make up your own sentence using the words or phrases given.

1. _____

(federal laws)

2. _____

(the people)

3. _____

(duty)

Dictation Practice

Write each sentence twice. For the first time, you can look at the sentence. For the second time, try writing the sentence without looking.

1. Congress is part of the American government.

2. Congress meets in Washington, D.C.

3. The House of Representative and Senate are parts of Congress.

4. There are 100 U.S. Senators.

5. Representatives are elected for two-year terms

1. _____

_____

2. _____

_____

3. _____

_____

4. _____

_____

5. _____

_____

THE EXECUTIVE BRANCH

The duty of the **executive branch** is to enforce the laws. At the federal level, the executive branch is the **president**, the **vice president**, the **cabinet**, and the departments under the cabinet members. The president signs bills into law and serves as **commander in chief** of the U.S. military. The cabinet is the special group that advises the president. The president's official home is the **White House**, which is in Washington, D.C.

As you remember from Lesson 1, we vote for the president in November, and the new president takes office in January. However, in order to run for president, a person must satisfy certain requirements as outlined in the Constitution: Candidates must (1) be a **natural-born citizen**, (2) be at least 35 years old, and (3) have lived in the United States for at least 14 years. The president is elected to a four-year term and may only serve two full terms. The Constitution also specifies the order of presidential succession. If the president should die, the vice president would become the next president. If both the president and the vice president should die, the Speaker of the House becomes president.

At the state level, the head executive is called a **governor**. At the city level, the head executive is called a **mayor**.

White House

Words to Know

Executive branch: the branch of government that enforces the laws
President: head executive at the federal level
Vice president: second in command at the federal level
Cabinet: special group that advises the president
Commander in chief: head executive of the military
White House: the president's official home
Natural-born citizen: citizen by birth in the United States
Governor: head executive at the state level
Mayor: head executive at the city level

Related Questions

1. Q: What is the executive branch?
   A: The executive branch is **the president, the vice president, the cabinet,** and **the departments under the cabinet members.**

2. Q: What is the job of the cabinet?
   A: The cabinet **advises the president.**

3. Q: Which branch enforces laws?
   A: The **executive branch** enforces laws.

4. Q: Who signs bills into laws and vetoes bills?
   A: **The president** signs bills into laws and vetoes bills.

5. Q: Who is the commander in chief of the U.S. military?
A: The president is the commander in chief of the U.S. military.

6. Q: How many full terms can a president serve?
A: A president can serve **two full terms**.

7. Q: Who becomes president of the United States if the president should die?
A: The vice president becomes president if the president should die.

8. Q: Who is the vice president of the United States today?
A: The current vice president is **Joe Biden**.

9. Q: Who is the president of the United States today?
A: The current president is **Barack Obama**.

10. Q: What is the political party of the president today?
A: The current president is a member of the **Democratic Party**.

11. Q: Who becomes president of the United States if both the president and the vice president should die?
A: The Speaker of the House would become president.

12. Q: Who is the Speaker of the House today?
A: Nancy Pelosi is the current Speaker of the House.

13. Q: For how long do we elect the president?
A: We elect the president for **four-year terms**.

14. Q: What is the White House?
A: The White House is **the president's official home**.

15. Q: During what month do we have elections for president?
A: We have elections in **November**.

16. Q: What is the head executive of a state government called?
A: The head executive of a state government is called a **governor**.

17. Q: Who is the governor of your state today?
A: The governor of my state is _____. (Look up your state's governor.)

18. Q: What is the head executive of a city government called?
A: The head executive of a city government is called a **mayor**.

The president leads the country

The governor leads the state

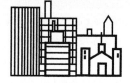

A mayor leads the city

Bonus Review

1. Q: Who elects the president of the United States?
A: The Electoral College elects of the president of the United States.

2. Q: In what month is the new president inaugurated?
A: The new president is inaugurated in **January**.

3. Q: Who was the first president of the United States?
A: George Washington was the first president of the United States.

4. Q: Who was president during the Civil War?
A: Abraham Lincoln was president during the Civil War.

5. Q: Which president was the first commander in chief?
A: George Washington was the first commander in chief.

6. Q: Who is your city's mayor?
A: The major of my city is _____. (Look up your city's mayor.)

Exercises

Fill in the Blank

The answers to these five questions can be found on page 112.

1. The _____ is the special group that advises the president.

2. The president is _____ of the U.S. military.

3. The _____ is the president's official home.

4. People vote for the president in _____ .

5. The _____ elects the president.

Sentence Composition

Make up your own sentence using the words or phrases given.

1. _____

    (vice president)

2. _____

    (White House)

3. _____

    (executive)

Multiple Choice

Choose the best answer for each question. Answers can be found on page 113.

1. How many terms is the president allowed to serve?
   a. four terms
   b. two terms
   c. one term
   d. unlimited terms.

2. In which month is the president inaugurated?
   a. January
   b. November
   c. July
   d. December

3. What does a mayor do?
   a. leads a state
   b. serves as a member of the president's cabinet
   c. leads a city
   d. serves in congress

Dictation Practice

Write each sentence twice. For the first time, you can look at the sentence. For the second time, try writing the sentence without looking.

1. People vote for the president in November.

2. The president signs bills into law.

3. The president has the power to veto.

4. The governor of my state is _____.

5. The cabinet advises the president.

1. _____

_____

2. _____

_____

3. _____

_____

4. _____

_____

5. _____

_____

12 ▶ THE JUDICIAL BRANCH

The **judicial branch** of the government interprets and explains the laws that Congress makes and the president enforces. At the federal level, the judicial branch is the **Supreme Court**, the highest court in the United States. The nine **Supreme Court justices** serve for life. The **chief justice** of the Supreme Court is the head justice. When there are openings on the Supreme Court, the president selects new Supreme Court justices.

Supreme Court

Words to Know

Judicial branch: the branch of government that interprets and explains the laws

Supreme Court: the highest court in the United States

Supreme Court justice: one of the nine judges on the Supreme Court

Chief justice: the head justice on the Supreme Court

Related Questions

1. Q: What does the judicial branch do?
   A: The judicial branch **reviews** and **interprets laws**, **resolves disputes**, and **determines if laws go against the Constitution**.

2. Q: Who is the chief justice of the Supreme Court today?
   A: **John Roberts** is the current chief justice of the Supreme Court.

3. Q: What is the highest court in the United States?
   A: **The Supreme Court** is the highest court in the United States.

4. Q: Who selects the Supreme Court justices?
   A: **The president** selects the Supreme Court justices.

5. Q: How many Supreme Court justices are there?
   A: There are **nine** Supreme Court justices.

Exercises

Fill in the Blank

The answers to these five questions can be found on page 113.

1. The _____ is the highest court in America.

2. The _____ is the branch of government that interprets the laws.

3. There are _____ Supreme Court justices.

4. The Supreme Court justices are appointed by _____.

5. Supreme Court justices serve for _____.

Sentence Composition

Make up your own sentence using the words or phrases given.

1. _____

(justice)

2. _____

(Supreme Court)

Dictation Practice

Write each sentence twice. For the first time, you can look at the sentence. For the second time, try writing the sentence without looking.

1. I am too busy to talk today.

2. My car does not work.

3. I count the cars as they pass by the office.

4. The judicial branch reviews and interprets laws.

5. The Supreme Court has a chief justice.

1. _____

   _____

2. _____

   _____

3. _____

   _____

4. _____

   _____

5. _____

   _____

SECTION REVIEW

The section review contains a useful list of important names and concepts that were covered in Section II. The lesson number of each concept is in parentheses

Following the review list is the official list of 100 questions, from which the interviewer at your citzenship interview will choose 10 to ask you. You will only be asked questions from the official list of 100. You should study these questions thoroughly after working through all of the exercises in Section II.

At the end of this review you will find the answer key, which lists all of the answers to the exercises in this book and the official 100 questions.

Study Aid

Here's a fun and effective study idea. Create flash cards to help you learn the official USCIS questions and answers. It's simple:

1. Buy index cards at your local paper goods or drug store.
2. Write a USCIS question on one side of each card and the correct answer on the back.
3. Shuffle the cards and have a friend or family member ask you the questions.
4. Keep trying until you get all of them right!

People

Abraham Lincoln (**8**)
American Indians (**6**)
Barack Obama (**11**)
Colonists (**6**)
Franklin D. Roosevelt (**8**)
George Washington (**7**)

Joe Biden (**11**)
Martin Luther King, Jr. (**8**)
Native Americans (**6**)
Natural-born citizen (**1**)
Naturalized citizen (**1**)
Nancy Pelosi (**11**)
Permanent resident (**1**)

Pilgrims (**6**)
Speaker of the House (**10**)
Thomas Jefferson (**7**)
Woodrow Wilson (**8**)
Terrorists (**8**)

Places

Canada (**4**)
Great Britain (**7**)
Louisiana territory (**8**)
Mexico (**4**)
Minnesota River (**4**)
Mississippi River (**4**)
United States of America (**1**)
U.S. Capitol building (**10**)
U.S. Territories (**4**)
Washington, D.C. (**3**)

Dates

July 4, 1776 (**7**)
1787 (**9**)
1861–1865 (**8**)

Wars

American Revolution (**7**)
Civil War (**8**)
Cold War (**8**)
Korean War (**8**)
Persian Gulf War (**8**)
Vietnam War (**8**)
World War I (**8**)
World War II (**8**)

Ideas

All men are created equal (**8**)
Checks and balances (**3**)
Religious freedom (**6**)
Right to vote (**1**)
Rule of law (**9**)
Speech, press, religion (**9**)

Documents

Amendments (**9**)
Bill of Rights (**9**)
Constitution (**9**)
Declaration of Independence (**7**)
Emancipation Proclamation (**8**)
Federalist papers (**7**)
N-400 (**1**)
Passport (**1**)

Other Important History and Events

13 original colonies (**6**)
50 states (**2**)
Civil rights movement (**8**)
Independence Day (**5**)
National holiday (**5**)
Slavery (**8**)
Thanksgiving (**5**)
"The Star-Spangled Banner" (**2**)

Government

Cabinet (**11**)
Commander in chief (**11**)
Congress (**10**)
Democrat (**1**)
Democratic Republic (**3**)
Electoral College (**1**)
Executive (**11**)
Governor (**11**)

House of Representatives (**10**)
Judicial branch (**12**)
Justices (**12**)
Legislative (**10**)
Limit (**10**)
Mayor (**11**)
Minimum voting age (**1**)
President (**11**)
Republican (**1**)

Senate (**10**)
Supreme Court (**12**)
Term (**10**)
USCIS (**1**)
Vice president (**11**)

The 100 Questions

The following is a list of the official USCIS civics and history questions. At your interview, you will be asked 10 questions from this list and you must answer at least six of them correctly.

There is an exception—applicants who are 65 years of age or older and have been legal permanent residents of the United States for at least 20 years are only tested on a subset of the questions. Those questions are marked on this list with an asterisk (*).

AMERICAN GOVERNMENT

A: Principles of American Democracy

1. What is the supreme law of the land?
2. What does the Constitution do?
3. The idea of self-government is in the first three words of the Constitution. What are these words?
4. What is an amendment?
5. What do we call the first ten amendments to the Constitution?
6. What is one right or freedom from the First Amendment?*
7. How many amendments does the Constitution have?
8. What did the Declaration of Independence do?
9. What are two rights in the Declaration of Independence?
10. What is freedom of religion?
11. What is the economic system in the United States?*
12. What is the "rule of law"?

B: System of Government

13. Name one branch or part of the government.*
14. What stops one branch of government from becoming too powerful?
15. Who is in charge of the executive branch?
16. Who makes federal laws?
17. What are the two parts of the U.S. Congress?*
18. How many U.S. senators are there?
19. We elect a U.S. senator for how many years?
20. Who is one of your state's U.S. senators now?*
21. The House of Representatives has how many voting members?
22. We elect a U.S. representative for how many years?
23. Who is one of your state's U.S. representatives?
24. Who does a U.S. senator represent?
25. Why do some states have more representatives than other states?
26. We elect a president for how many years?
27. In what month do we vote for president?*
28. What is the name of the president of the United States now?*
29. What is the name of the vice president of the United States now?
30. If the president can no longer serve, who becomes president?
31. If both the president and the vice president can no longer serve, who becomes president?

32. Who is the commander in chief of the military?

33. Who signs bills to become laws?

34. Who vetoes bills?

35. What does the president's cabinet do?

36. What are two cabinet-level positions?

37. What does the judicial branch do?

38. What is the highest court in the United States?

39. How many justices are on the Supreme Court?

40. Who is the chief justice of the United States now?

41. Under our Constitution, some powers belong to the federal government. What is one power of the federal government?

42. Under our Constitution, some powers belong to the states. What is one power of the states?

43. Who is the governor of your state now?

44. What is the capital of your state?*

45. What are the two major political parties in the United States?*

46. What is the political party of the president now?

47. What is the name of the speaker of the House of Representatives now?

C: Rights and Responsibilities

48. There are four amendments to the Constitution about who can vote. Describe one of them.

49. What is one responsibility that is only for United States citizens?*

50. Name one right only for United States citizens.

51. What are two rights of everyone living in the United States?

52. What do we show loyalty to when we say the Pledge of Allegiance?

53. What is one promise you make when you become a United States citizen?

54. How old do citizens have to be to vote for president?*

55. What are two ways that Americans can participate in their democracy?

56. When is the last day you can send in federal income tax forms?*

57. When must all men register for the Selective Service?

AMERICAN HISTORY

A: Colonial Period and Independence

58. What is one reason colonists came to America?

59. Who lived in America before the Europeans arrived?

60. What group of people was taken to America and sold as slaves?

61. Why did the colonists fight the British?

62. Who wrote the Declaration of Independence?

63. When was the Declaration of Independence adopted?

64. There were 13 original states. Name three.

65. What happened at the Constitutional Convention?

66. When was the Constitution written?

67. The Federalist Papers supported the passage of the U.S. Constitution. Name one of the writers.

68. What is one thing Benjamin Franklin is famous for?

69. Who is the "Father of Our Country"?

70. Who was the first President?*

B: 1800s

71. What territory did the United States buy from France in 1803?

72. Name one war fought by the United States in the 1800s.

73. Name the U.S. war between the north and the south.

74. Name one problem that led to the Civil War.

75. What was one important thing that Abraham Lincoln did?*

76. What did the Emancipation Proclamation do?

77. What did Susan B. Anthony do?

C: Recent American History and Other Important Historical Information

78. Name one war fought by the United States in the 1900s.*

79. Who was President during World War I?

80. Who was President during the Great Depression and World War II?

81. Who did the United States fight in World War II?

82. Before he was President, Eisenhower was a general. What war was he in?

83. During the Cold War, what was the main concern of the United States?

84. What movement tried to end racial discrimination?

85. What did Martin Luther King, Jr. do?*

86. What major event happened on September 11, 2001, in the United States?

87. Name one American Indian tribe in the United States.

INTEGRATED CIVICS

A: Geography

88. Name one of the two longest rivers in the United States.

89. What ocean is on the West Coast of the United States?

90. What ocean is on the East Coast of the United States?

91. Name one U.S. territory.

92. Name one state that borders Canada.

93. Name one state that borders Mexico.

94. What is the capital of the United States?*

95. Where is the Statue of Liberty?*

B: Symbols

96. Why does the flag have 13 stripes?

97. Why does the flag have 50 stars?*

98. What is the name of the national anthem?

C: Holidays

99. When do we celebrate Independence Day?*

100. Name two national U.S. holidays.

Answers

Lesson 1
Fill in the Blank
1. The president of the United States is elected by the <u>Electoral College.</u>
2. You must be at least <u>18</u> years old to vote in the United States.
3. The two major political parties in America are the <u>Democratic</u> and the <u>Republican</u> parties.
4. The right to <u>vote</u> is the most important right granted to American citizens.
5. Congress is directly <u>elected</u> by the people.

Multiple Choice
1. c
2. a
3. c

Lesson 2
Fill in the Blank
1. The colors of the flag are <u>red</u>, <u>white</u>, and <u>blue.</u>
2. The stars on the flag represent <u>the 50 states in the union.</u>
3. The <u>stripes</u> on the flag represent the 13 original colonies.
4. Our national anthem is called <u>"The Star-Spangled Banner."</u>

Multiple Choice
1. b
2. d
3. b

Lesson 3
Fill in the Blank
1. The head executive of a state is a <u>governor.</u>
2. The <u>legislative</u> branch of government makes the federal laws.
3. <u>Washington, D.C.</u> is the capital of the United States of America.
4. The system of government of the United States in which citizens elect representatives to govern them is a <u>democratic republic.</u>
5. The <u>president</u>, the vice president, and the <u>cabinet</u> make up the executive branch.

Multiple Choice
1. c
2. c
3. d

Lesson 4
Fill in the Blank
1. The United States is bordered by <u>Canada</u> to the north and <u>Mexico</u> to the south.
2. Guam and Puerto Rico are examples of United States <u>territories.</u>
3. The Mississippi and the Missouri are the country's two longest <u>rivers.</u>
4. Minnesota is a state that borders <u>Canada.</u>
5. California is a state that borders <u>Mexico.</u>

Multiple Choice
1. b
2. c
3. b

Lesson 5
Fill in the Blank
1. The important holiday on July 4 is <u>Independence Day.</u>
2. Thanksgiving, Veterans Day, and Memorial Day are all examples of <u>national holidays.</u>

Lesson 6
Fill in the Blank
1. The <u>pilgrims</u> were the first American colonists.
2. The 13 original states were called <u>colonies.</u>
3. The <u>Native Americans (American Indians)</u> lived in America before the colonists arrived.
4. <u>Thanksgiving</u> is the holiday that was first celebrated by the American colonists.
5. The pilgrims came to America for <u>religious freedom.</u>

Lesson 7
Fill in the Blank
1. The Declaration of Independence was adopted on <u>July 4, 1776.</u>
2. Alexander Hamilton and John Jay were two of the writers of <u>the Federalist Papers.</u>
3. The oldest member of the Constitutional Convention was <u>Benjamin Franklin.</u>
4. The main writer of the Declaration of Independence was <u>Thomas Jefferson.</u>
4. <u>George Washington</u> was the first commander in chief of the U.S. Army.
5. One of the main beliefs of the <u>Declaration of Independence</u> is that all men are created equal.

Multiple Choice
1. c
2. b
3. a

Lesson 8
Fill in the Blank
1. The United States purchased the <u>Louisiana Territory</u> from France in 1803.
2. In <u>the Civil War</u>, the northern states of the United States fought against the southern states and won.
3. The primary reason for the Civil War was <u>slavery.</u>
4. Abraham Lincoln's <u>Emancipation Proclamation</u> freed the slaves.
5. The president of the United States during World War II was <u>Franklin Delano Roosevelt (FDR).</u>
6. The <u>civil rights</u> movement worked to end discrimination.
7. On September 11, 2001, <u>terrorists</u> attacked the United States.

Multiple Choice
1. b
2. a
3. c

Lesson 9
Fill in the Blank
1. The <u>Constitution</u> is the supreme law of the land.
2. The <u>Preamble</u> is the introduction to the Constitution.
3. There have been 27 <u>amendments</u> to the Constitution.
4. The first ten amendments are called the <u>Bill of Rights.</u>
5. Freedom of <u>speech / press / religion</u> is guaranteed by one of the ten amendments.
6. <u>"We the people"</u> are the first three words of the Preamble.

Lesson 10
Fill in the Blank
1. Congress is made up of the <u>Senate</u> and the <u>House of Representatives.</u>
2. Only <u>Congress</u> has the power to declare war.
3. Congress meets in the U.S. <u>Capitol</u> building.
4. We elect each <u>representative</u> for two-year terms.
5. There is no limit to how many <u>terms</u> a senator or representative may serve.
6. States with larger populations have <u>more</u> U.S. representatives.

Lesson 11
Fill in the Blank
1. The <u>cabinet</u> is the special group that advises the president.
2. The president is <u>commander in chief</u> of the U.S. military.
3. The <u>White House</u> is the president's official home.
4. People vote for the president in <u>November.</u>
5. The <u>Electoral College</u> elects the president.

Multiple Choice
1. b
2. a
3. c

Lesson 12
Fill in the Blank
1. The <u>Supreme Court</u> is the highest court in America.
2. The <u>judicial branch</u> is the branch of government that interprets the laws.
3. There are <u>nine</u> Supreme Court justices.
4. The Supreme Court justices are appointed by <u>the president.</u>
5. Supreme Court justices serve for <u>life.</u>

Answers to the 100 Questions

1. The Constitution

2. Possible answers:
   • sets up the government
   • defines the government
   • protects basic rights of Americans

3. We the People

4. A change or an addition (to the Constitution)

5. The Bill of Rights

6. Possible answers:
   • religion
   • assembly
   • press
   • petition the government

7. Twenty-seven (27)

8. Announced (or declared) our independence (from Great Britain)

9. Possible answers:
   • life
   • liberty
   • pursuit of happiness

10. You can practice any religion, or not practice a religion.

11. Capitalist economy or market economy

12. Possible variations:
    • Everyone must follow the law.
    • Leaders must obey the law.
    • Government must obey the law.
    • No one is above the law.

13. Possible answers:
    • Congress
    • legislative
    • president
    • executive
    • the courts
    • judicial

14. Checks and balances or separation of powers

15. The President

16. Possible answers:
    • Congress
    • Senate and House of Representatives
    • (U.S. or national) legislature

17. The Senate and House of Representatives

18. One hundred (100)

19. Six (6)

20. Look up your state senator

21. Four hundred thirty-five (435)

22. Two (2)

23. Look up your representative

24. All people of the state

25. Possible answers:
- (because of) the state's population
- (because) they have more people
- (because) some states have more people

26. Four (4)

27. November

28. Barack Obama or President Obama

29. Joe Biden or Vice President Biden

30. The vice president

31. The speaker of the House

32. The president

33. The president

34. The president

35. Advises the president

36. Possible answers:
- secretary of agriculture
- secretary of commerce
- secretary of defense
- secretary of education
- secretary of energy
- secretary of health and human services
- secretary of homeland security
- secretary of housing and urban development
- secretary of the interior
- secretary of labor
- secretary of state
- secretary of transportation
- secretary of the treasury
- secretary of veterans affairs
- attorney general
- vice president

37. Possible variations:
- reviews laws
- explains laws
- resolves disputes (disagreements)
- decides if a law goes against the Constitution

38. The Supreme Court

39. Nine (9)

40. John Roberts or Chief Justice Roberts

41. Possible answers:
- to print money
- to declare war
- to create an army
- to make treaties

42. Possible answers:
- provide schooling and education
- provide protection (police)
- provide safety (fire departments)
- give a driver's license
- approve zoning and land use

43. Look up your governor

44. Look up the capital of your state

45. Democratic and Republican

46. Democratic

47. Nancy Pelosi or Speaker Pelosi

48. Possible answers:
- citizens eighteen (18) and older can vote
- you don't have to pay a poll tax to vote

- any citizen can vote
- a male citizen of any race can vote

49. Possible answers:
- serve on a jury
- vote in a federal election

50. Run for federal office

51. Possible answers:
- freedom of expression
- freedom of speech
- freedom of assembly
- freedom to petition the government
- freedom of worship
- the right to bear arms

52. The United States or the flag

53. Possible answers:
- give up loyalty to other countries
- defend the Constitution and laws of the United States
- obey the laws of the United States
- serve in the U.S. military (if needed)
- serve the nation (if needed)
- be loyal to the United States

54. Eighteen (18) and older

55. Possible answers:
- vote
- join a political party
- help with a campaign
- join a civic group
- join a community group
- give an elected official your opinion on an issue
- call senators and representatives
- publicly support or oppose an issue or policy
- run for office
- write to a newspaper

56. April 15

57. between eighteen (18) and twenty-six (26)

58. Possible answers:
- freedom
- political liberty
- religious freedom
- economic opportunity
- practice their religion
- escape persecution

59. American Indians or Native Americans

60. people from Africa

61. Possible answers:
- because of high taxes (taxation without representation)
- because the British army stayed in their houses (boarding, quartering)
- because they didn't have self-government

62. Thomas Jefferson

63. July 4, 1776

64. Possible answers:
- Connecticut
- Delaware
- Georgia
- Maryland
- Massachusetts
- New Hampshire
- New Jersey
- New York
- North Carolina
- Pennsylvania
- Rhode Island
- South Carolina
- Virginia

65. The Constitution was written

66. 1787

67. Possible answers:
- Alexander Hamilton
- James Madison
- John Jay
- Publius

68. Possible answers:
- U.S. diplomat
- oldest member of the Constitutional Convention
- first Postmaster General of the United States
- writer of *Poor Richard's Almanac*
- started the first free libraries

69. George Washington

70. George Washington

71. The Louisiana Territory

72. Possible answers:
- War of 1812
- Mexican-American War
- Civil War
- Spanish-American War

73. The Civil War

74. Possible answers:
- slavery
- economic reasons
- states' rights

75. Possible answers:
- freed the slaves (Emancipation Proclamation)
- saved (preserved) the union
- led the United States during the Civil War

76. freed the slaves

77. fought for women's rights or civil rights

78. Possible answers:
- World War I
- World War II
- Korean War
- Vietnam War
- Persian Gulf War

79. Woodrow Wilson

80. Franklin Roosevelt

81. Japan, Germany, and Italy

82. World War II

83. communism

84. Civil Rights Movement

85. fought for civil rights and equality for all Americans

86. terrorists attacked the United States

87. Possible answers:
- Apache
- Arawak
- Blackfeet
- Cherokee
- Cheyenne
- Chippewa
- Choctaw
- Creek
- Crow
- Hopi
- Huron
- Inuit
- Iroquois
- Lakota
- Mohegan
- Navajo
- Oneida
- Pueblo
- Seminole
- Shawnee
- Sioux
- Teton

88. Missouri River and Mississippi River

89. Pacific Ocean

90. Atlantic Ocean

91. Possible answers:
- American Samoa
- Guam
- Northern Mariana Islands
- Puerto Rico
- U.S. Virgin Islands

92. Possible answers:
- Maine
- New Hampshire
- Vermont
- New York
- Pennsylvania
- Ohio
- Michigan
- Minnesota
- North Dakota
- Montana
- Idaho
- Washington
- Alaska

93. Possible answers:
- California
- Arizona
- New Mexico
- Texas

94. Washington, D.C.

95. Possible answers:
- New York Harbor
- Liberty Island
- New Jersey
- Near New York City
- On the Hudson River

96. because there were 13 original colonies

97. because there is one star for each state

98. The Star-Spangled Banner

99. July 4

100. Possible answers:
- New Year's Day
- Martin Luther King, Jr. Day
- Presidents' Day
- Memorial Day
- Independence Day
- Labor Day
- Columbus Day
- Veterans Day
- Thanksgiving
- Christmas

The U.S. Citizenship Exam is given in the form of an interview. It is often referred to as a citizenship interview, naturalization interview, naturalization test, or citizenship exam. This section will walk you through the steps of the actual citizenship interview. Each chapter covers a different stage of the interview process. Work slowly and carefully through each lesson, and practice with all the exercises. The section review at the end of the section revisits some of the key questions.

Here's an outline of what's in this section:

Before You Begin

The key to the interview process is to understand what your interviewer is asking you. If you don't hear what he or she says, it is better to ask your interviewer to repeat the question than to guess what question was asked. Stay calm, and listen carefully to catch the important words in each question. The first word is often very important, and even one syllable can make a difference, such as this: **When were you born?** vs. **Where were you born?** The first question asks for the date of your birth, while the second question asks for the place of your birth.

Here are a few tips to keep in mind during the interview process:

- Stay calm!
- Identify the key question words.
- Think carefully about your answer.
- And remember these useful phrases:
  - **Please repeat that.**
  - **Please speak more slowly.**
  - **Please speak louder.**

What to Bring to Your Interview

You should bring all of the following documents with you to your interview—both originals and a copy of each for the interviewer to keep with your records. These documents should be original or certified copies and in English. If your documents are not in English, a certified translator must translate them and they must be marked as such. Translators cannot be an interested party, friend, or family member.

- Photo identification
- Permanent resident card
- Passport
- Any travel documents issued by the USCIS
- Copies of your tax returns from the past five years
- Selective Service registration card
- Any arrest reports, certified court dispositions, or probation reports that you might have
- If you have arranged to take an alternate Oath of Allegiance for religious reasons, you should bring supporting documents (such as a letter from your religious organization)

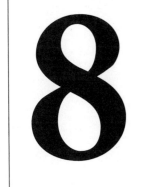

CHAPTER

THE PRE-INTERVIEW

Even before your actual interview starts, the interviewer will get an idea of your English-speaking level through greetings and small talk. Be prepared to start answering questions as soon as you enter the testing room. Just before the formal interview, you will be asked to take a truth oath, and your interviewer will check your identity. This chapter will prepare you for each of these steps so that you can focus on the actual interview itself.

13 ▶ GREETINGS AND SMALL TALK

At the USCIS testing facility, the interviewer will call your name and lead you to an office. Before starting the actual interview, he or she will begin with some general conversation, or small talk, to see how well you speak English. If the interviewer feels that he or she cannot successfully communicate with you in English, the interview may be ended. Here are some questions that the interviewer might ask you, along with sample answers.

"How Are You?" Questions

Q: How are you?
A: <u>I am fine / good / great.</u> OR <u>Fine / Good, thank you.</u>

Q: How is the weather today?
A: The weather is <u>fine / good / cold / warm / sunny / rainy / windy.</u> (Pick which one applies.)

Q: How did you get here today?
A: I came by <u>car / bus / subway / train.</u> OR <u>My son / daughter brought me.</u>

Why You Are Here

Q: Do you understand why you are here today?
A: <u>Yes</u>

Q: Why are you here today?
A: <u>For my citizenship interview.</u> OR <u>Because I want to be a U.S. citizen.</u>

Q: Why do you want to become a U.S. citizen?
A: <u>Because I love America.</u> (Use your own reason!)

Beginning the Interview

Q: Do you have any questions before we begin?
A: <u>No</u>

Preparation and Study

Q: Have you prepared for the citizenship test?
A: <u>Yes</u>

Q: Have you studied for the citizenship test?
A: <u>Yes</u>

Q: How did you study / prepare?
A: <u>I read a book.</u> OR <u>I took a class.</u> OR <u>My children helped me.</u>

14 ▶ TRUTH OATH AND IDENTITY CHECK

N ow the interviewer will ask you to take the truth oath. He or she will ask you to swear that you will tell the truth during the interview. Here is what you may hear. Say these phrases out loud several times.

Interviewer: "Okay, let's begin. Please stand and raise your right hand."

What you do: Get out of your chair and put your right hand in the air.

What it means: You are getting ready to take an oath, or promise.

Interviewer: "Do you promise to tell the truth and nothing but the truth so help you God?" OR "Do you swear that everything you say today will be the truth?"

What you do: Answer out loud, "<u>Yes.</u>"

What it means: You promise to tell the truth. You promise to tell no lies.

Interviewer: "Please sit down." OR "You can sit down now."

What you do: Sit down in your chair again.

What it means: The oath is finished.

Extra Practice

Q: Do you understand what an oath is?

A: <u>Yes, it is a promise to tell the truth.</u>

The interviewer will then check your identity, and you will have to show your verification information, such as the Appointment Notice and alien registration card.

Interviewer: "At this point, I have to check your identity. I need to see your **Appointment Notice** or **Invitation to Appear**. I would also like to see your passport if you have one, and your **alien registration card.**

What you do: Show the letter you received in the mail from USCIS, which is called your **Appointment Notice** or **Invitation to Appear**. Then show your **alien registration card.**

What it means: You can prove who you are.

After the interviewer has checked your identity, the actual interview will begin.

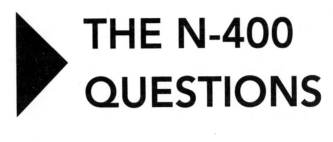

CHAPTER 9 ▶ THE N-400 QUESTIONS

Verifying and going over your N-400 form will be an important part of your citizenship interview. This chapter will help familiarize you with your information and how your interviewer may ask questions about your information. Have a partner read the questions listed in each lesson out loud to you so you can practice answering them.

GENERAL INFORMATION

Your interviewer will go through your N-400 form to check the information you wrote. Be sure to keep a copy of your N-400 form to review the answers to all the following questions.

N-400 Parts 1 & 2:
Your Name and Information about Your Eligibility

Q: What is your name?
A: My name is _____ .

Q: Spell your last name.
A: __ - __ - __ - __ - __ - __ - __ - __ - __ - __ - __ - __ - __

Q: When did you first come to the United States?
A: I came to the United States on _____ (month, day, year).

Q: How long have you been a permanent resident?
A: _____ years

Q: Have you ever used a different name?
A: <u>Yes</u> / <u>No</u>

Q: Do you want to change your name?
A: <u>Yes</u> / <u>No</u> (If yes, say what you want to change it to.)

Q: To what do you want to change your name? OR What name do you want to have now?
A: _____.

Q: What other names have you gone by? OR What other names have you used in the past?
A: _____ OR <u>None.</u>

Q: What was your maiden name?
A: Before I was married, my name was _____.

N-400 Part 3: Information about You

Q: How long have you been a permanent resident of the United States? OR How long have you lived in the United States?
A: _____ years

Q: When did you become a permanent resident? OR When did you first come to the United States? OR On what date did you enter the United States?
A: _____ (month, day, year)

Q: You've been a permanent resident since _____, is that correct?
A: <u>Yes</u> (If no, say the correct date.)

Q: Where did you enter the United States? OR What was your port of entry? OR In what port of entry did you arrive in America?
A: _____.

Q: What is your date of birth? OR What is your birthday? OR When were you born?
A: I was born on _____ (month, day, year).

Q: What is your country of birth? OR Where were you born?
A: I was born in _____ (country).

Q: What is your nationality? OR What is your current citizenship?

A: I am _____ (nationality).

Q: What is your Social Security number?

    NOTE: You might NOT want to write your Social Security number in this book, but it is a very good idea to memorize it.

A: My Social Security number is __ __ __ - __ __ - __ __ __ __ .

Q: What is your marital status?

A: I am <u>single / married / divorced / widowed.</u>

Q: Are you married?

A: <u>Yes</u> / <u>No</u>

Q: Have you ever been divorced?

A: <u>Yes</u> / <u>No</u>

Q: Was your marriage annulled?

A: <u>Yes</u> / <u>No</u>

Q: How long have you been married?

A: I have been married for _____ years.

N-400 Part 4: Addresses and Telephone Numbers

Q: What is your home address? OR Where do you live?

A: I live at _____ .

Q: What is your home phone number? OR What is your telephone number at home?

A: My phone number is __ __ __-__ __ __-__ __ __ __ .

Q: Do you have a work telephone number?

A: <u>Yes</u> / <u>No</u> OR No, I am not currently working.

Q: What is your work phone number?

A: My work phone number is __ __ __-__ __ __-__ __ __ __ .

Q: What is your e-mail address?

A: My e-mail address is _____ .

N-400 Part 5: Information for Criminal Records Search

Q: What is your height? OR How tall are you?
A: I am _____ feet, _____ inches tall.

Q: What is your weight? OR How much do you weigh?
A: I weigh _____ pounds.

Q: Are you Hispanic? OR Are you Latino/a?
A: <u>Yes</u> / <u>No</u>

Q: What is your race?
A: I am <u>White / Asian / Black or African American / American Indian or Alaskan Native / Native Hawaiian or Other Pacific Islander / Other:</u> _____.

Q: What is your hair color? OR What color is your hair?
A: My hair is <u>black / brown / blonde / gray / white / red / sandy / other:</u> _____. OR I am bald.

Q: What is your eye color?
A: My eyes are <u>brown / blue / green / hazel / gray / black / other:</u> _____.

16 ▶ MORE DETAILED INFORMATION

Your interviewer may ask you to answer the following questions with detailed information. Or, your interviewer may also just read off your N-400 form and ask you if that information is right. Be sure to know all the information on your N-400 form thoroughly. If your information changes after you mail in your N-400 form, be ready to explain the changes.

N-400 Part 6: Information about Your Residence and Employment

Q: Where have you lived in the past five years?
A: I have lived at _____ (list all addresses beginning with your current address).

Q: Are these all the places you have lived in the last five years?
A: Yes / No (If no, explain why you did not write it on the form.)

Q: Have you lived in any other places in the last five years?
A: Yes / No (If yes, explain why you did not write it on the form.)

Q: Have you worked in the last five years?
A: <u>Yes</u> / <u>No</u>

Q: Are you currently employed? OR Do you have a job?
A: <u>Yes</u> / <u>No</u>

Q: Why aren't you working?
A: I am not working because _____ . (Be honest!)

Q: What is your occupation? OR What do you do? OR What kind of work do you do?
A: I am / was a _____ . OR I am retired.

Q: Where do you work? OR Who do you work for? OR Who is your employer? OR How do you support yourself?
A: I work at _____ .

Q: How long have you worked there? OR How long have you held this job?
A: I have worked there for _____ years.

Q: Who was your employer before that?
A: _____ .

Q: Please list your employers in the past five years.
A: I have worked for _____ (list all employers).

Q: Is this list of employers complete?
A: <u>Yes</u> / <u>No</u> (If no, explain why you did not write it on the form.)

N-400 Part 7: Time outside the United States

Q: Since becoming a permanent resident, have you ever left the United States? OR Have you left the United States since you became a permanent resident? OR Since coming to the United States, have you traveled to any other country? OR Have you visited any other country since becoming a permanent resident?
A: <u>Yes</u> / <u>No</u>

Q: How many times have you left the United States since you became a permanent resident?
A: _____ times

Q: How long were you away?
A: I was gone for _____ <u>days / weeks / months / years.</u>

Q: What country did you travel to? OR Where did you go?
A: I went to _____ .

Q: Why did you leave the United States?
A: I left because _____ .

Q: Did any of these trips last six months or more?
A: <u>Yes</u> / <u>No</u> (If yes, be prepared to explain why.)

Q: When was your most recent trip? OR When was the last time you left the United States?
A: It was _____ .

Q: For how long were you in _____ (country)?
A: I was there for _____ <u>days / weeks / months / years.</u>

N-400 Part 8: Information about Your Marital History

The following questions ask about your marital status. If you have never been married, you do not need to review this section. Skip to Part 9 on page 136.

Q: What is your marital status?
A: I am <u>single / married / divorced / widowed.</u>

Q: Have you ever been married?
A: <u>Yes</u> / <u>No</u>

Q: Are you married?
A: <u>Yes</u> / <u>No</u>

Q: How many times have you been married?
A: I have been married _____ times.

Q: What is the full name of your husband / wife?
A: My husband's / wife's name is _____ .

Q: What is your husband's / wife's date of birth?
A: __ __ / __ __ / __ __ __ __

Q: When did you marry him / her?
A: __ __ / __ __ / __ __ __ __

Q: What is his / her current address?
A: _____ .

Q: Is your husband / wife a U.S. citizen?
A: <u>Yes</u> / <u>No</u>

Q: What is his / her immigration status?
A: He / she is a permanent resident. OR He / she is a U.S. citizen.

Q: What is his / her country of citizenship?
A: _____ .

Q: When did he / she become a U.S. citizen?
A: __ __ / __ __ / __ __ __ __ .

Q: If your husband / wife is NOT a U.S. citizen, what is his / her country of origin?
A: He / she is from _____ .

Q: If your husband / wife is NOT a U.S. citizen, what is his / her USCIS "A" number?
A: His / her USCIS "A" number is _____ .

Q: Has your current spouse been married before
A: <u>Yes</u> / <u>No</u>

Q: Have you ever been divorced?
A: <u>Yes</u> / <u>No</u>

Q: Why did you get a divorce?
A: _____ .

N-400 Part 9: Information about Your Children

Q: How many children do you have? OR How many sons and daughters do you have?
A: _____

Q: What are the full names of your sons and daughters?
A: (Say each child's first, middle, and last name.)

Q: Do your children live with you?
A: <u>Yes</u> / <u>No</u>

Q: How many people live in your house?

A: _____ people: myself, <u>my husband / wife,</u> and _____ children.

Q: Who do you live with?

A: I live with _____ .

Q: Where do your children live?

A: My children live with me in _____ . OR Other: _____ .

Q: Did any of your children stay in your native country?

A: <u>Yes</u> / <u>No</u>

Q: When were your children born?

A: One was born in _____ , one in _____ ,

and one in _____ (or more).

Q: Were they all born in the United States?

A: <u>Yes</u> / <u>No</u>

LESSON

17 ▶ ADDITIONAL QUESTIONS

The following questions are all yes or no questions. Pay attention to the beginning of each question, because that will give you a clue about how to answer it. However, make sure you know what each question is asking.

SENTENCE PATTERNS

For questions beginning with:	Answer:
"Have you ever..."	No
"Did you ever..."	No
"Do you owe..."	No
"Do you believe..."	Yes
"Do you support..."	Yes
"If the law requires it, are you willing..."	Yes

General Questions

Q: **Have you ever** claimed (in writing or in any other way) to be a U.S. citizen? OR **Have you ever** pretended to be a U.S. citizen?

Q: **Have you ever** registered to vote in any federal, state, or local election in the United States? OR **Have you ever** voted in any federal, state, or local election in the United States?

Q: Since becoming a lawful permanent resident, **have you ever** failed to file a required federal, state, or local tax return? OR **Do you owe** any federal, state, or local taxes that are overdue?

Q: Do you have any title of nobility in any foreign country? OR Were you born with or have you acquired any title of nobility? OR Are you a king, queen, duke, earl, prince, or princess, or do you have any other title of nobility?

Q: **Have you ever** been declared legally incompetent or been confined to a mental institution within the last five years? OR **Have you ever** been in a mental hospital? OR **Have you ever** been confined as a patient in a mental institution?

A: <u>No</u> (If yes, explain.)

Affiliations

Q: **Have you ever** been affiliated with any organization, association, fund, foundation, party, club, or society in the United States or in any other place?

Q: **Have you ever** been a member of the communist party?

Q: **Have you ever** been a member of any other totalitarian party?

Q: **Have you ever** been a member of a terrorist organization?

Q: **Have you ever** advocated the overthrow of any government by force or violence?

Q: **Have you ever** persecuted any person because of race, religion, national origin, membership in a particular social group, or political opinion?

Q: **Have you ever** worked for or been associated with the Nazi government of Germany or any government in any place that was occupied by, allied with, or established with the help of the Nazi government?

A: <u>No</u> (If yes, explain why.)

Continuous Residence

Q: **Have you ever** called yourself a "nonresident" on a federal, state, or local tax return?

Q: **Have you ever** failed to file a federal, state, or local tax return because you considered yourself to be a nonresident?

A: <u>No</u> (If yes, explain why.)

Paying Taxes

Q: **Have you ever** failed to file a federal income tax return?

Q: Was there ever a year when you didn't file your federal tax forms?

A: <u>No</u> (If you have failed to file taxes, say "yes" and explain why.)

Q: Have you filed your federal taxes every year?

Q: Do you pay taxes?

A: <u>Yes</u> (If you have not filed federal taxes every year, say "no" and explain why.)

Military Service

Q: **Have you ever** served in the U.S. Armed Forces?

Q: **Have you ever** left the United States to avoid being drafted into the U.S. Armed Forces? OR **Have you ever** left the United States so you didn't have to fight in a war?

Q: **Have you ever** applied for any kind of exemption from military service in the U.S. Armed Forces?

Q: **Have you ever** deserted from the U.S Armed Forces?

Q: **Have you ever** failed to comply with Selective Service laws?

Q: **Have you ever** tried to avoid military service?

A: <u>No</u>

Removal, Exclusion, and Deportation Proceedings

Q: Are removal, exclusion, rescission, or deportation proceedings pending against you?

Q: **Have you ever** been removed, excluded, or deported from the United States?

Q: **Have you ever** been ordered to be removed, excluded, or deported from the United States?

Q: **Have you ever** applied for any kind of relief from removal, exclusion, or deportation?

A: <u>No</u>

18 ▶ GOOD MORAL CHARACTER

In order to be eligible for citizenship, you must be a person of good moral character. Moral character is one of the attributes that make up and distinguish an individual. Your interviewer will ask a series of questions to determine whether or not you have a good moral character. This lesson includes questions that ask about your moral character. The answers to these questions are usually "no," but be sure to understand what each question is asking. Read them carefully and learn the definitions of the key words that follow.

While the answers listed below for all of the questions pertaining to moral character is "no," your situation may be different. If you must answer "yes" to any of the questions, be prepared to explain your answer. For example, your interviewer may ask you what the outcome of your detainment was if you answered "yes" to whether or not you were ever detained by a law enforcement official. Be sure to answer all questions about your moral character honestly.

Q: Have you ever committed a **crime** or **offense** for which you were not arrested?
A: No, I have never committed a crime and have never been arrested.

Q: Have you ever been **arrested**, **cited**, or **detained** by any law enforcement officer for any reason?
A: <u>No</u>, I have never been arrested, cited, or detained.

Q: Have you ever been **charged** with committing any crime or offense?
A: <u>No</u>, I have never been charged with a crime.

Q: Have you ever been **convicted** of a crime or offense?
A: <u>No</u>, I have never been convicted of a crime.

Q: Have you ever been placed in an **alternative sentencing** or a **rehabilitative program**?
A: <u>No</u>, I have not.

Q: Have you ever received a **suspended sentence**, been placed on **probation**, or been **paroled**?
A: <u>No</u>, I have not.

Q: Have you ever been in **jail** or **prison**?
A: <u>No</u>, I have never been in jail or prison.

Q: Have you ever been a **habitual drunkard**? OR Were you ever drunk every day?
A: <u>No</u>, I drink only a little. OR No, I don't drink alcohol.

Q: Have you ever advocated or practiced **polygamy**? OR Have you ever been married to more than one person at the same time?
A: <u>No</u>

Q: Have you ever been a **prostitute**? OR Have you ever sold your body for money?
A: <u>No</u>, I've never taken money for sex.

Q: Have you ever knowingly and for gain helped any alien to enter the United States illegally? OR Have you ever **smuggled** anyone into the United States? OR Have you ever accepted money for sneaking someone into the United States?
A: <u>No</u>, I have never helped anyone enter the United States illegally.

Q: Have you ever bought or sold **illegal drugs**? OR Have you ever been a trafficker in illegal drugs? OR Have you ever carried illegal drugs for someone else? OR Have you ever been a trafficker in cocaine or crack? OR Have you ever bought or sold marijuana or speed?
A: <u>No</u>, I have never bought or sold illegal drugs.

Q: Have you ever received income from illegal **gambling**? OR Did you ever get money illegally from gambling? OR Have you ever received money from illegal gambling? OR Have you ever received money or other goods from illegal gambling?
A: <u>No</u>, I don't gamble.

Words to Know

Habitual drunkard: person who drinks too much alcohol

Polygamy: having more than one husband or wife at the same time

Prostitute: to sell your body for money

Smuggle: illegally sneaking someone into the country

Illegal drugs: drugs that are produced, distributed and/or possessed in an unlicensed, or illegal way

Gamble: play games for money

19 ▶ OATH REQUIREMENTS

These last six questions will almost certainly be asked at your interview, because they are the requirements for the Oath of Allegiance to the United States. The answer to all of these questions should be "yes" if you want to become an American citizen, but be sure you know what each question means. Study the questions and vocabulary, and then read the full Oath of Allegiance that follows. If you pass your interview, the interviewer will ask you to read the Oath of Allegiance and sign your name. You should become familiar with the oath prior to your interview.

Q: 1. Do you support the **Constitution** and form of government of the United States?

2. Do you understand the full **Oath of Allegiance** to the United States?

3. Are you willing to take the full Oath of Allegiance to the United States?

4. If the law requires it, are you willing to **bear arms** on behalf of the United States?

5. If the law requires it, are you willing to perform **noncombatant services** in the U.S. Armed Forces?

6. If the law requires it, are you willing to perform work of national importance under civilian direction?

A: Yes

Words and Phrases to Know

Constitution: the supreme law of the land
Oath: a promise
Oath of Allegiance: promise to be loyal to the United States
Bear arms: fight for the United States
Noncombatant services: work for the United States, but not fight

Oath of Allegiance

I hereby declare, on oath, that I absolutely and entirely renounce and abjure all allegiance and fidelity to any foreign prince, potentate, state, or sovereignty, of whom or which I have heretofore been a subject or citizen; that I will support and defend the Constitution and laws of the United States when required by law; that I will bear true faith and allegiance to the same; that I will bear arms on behalf of the United States when required by law; that I will perform noncombatant service in the Armed Forces of the United States when required by law; that I will perform work of national importance under civilian direction when required by law; and that I take this obligation freely, without any mental reservation or purpose of evasion; so help me God.

LANGUAGE AND KNOWLEDGE ASSESSMENT

During your interview, you will also be asked to show that you can read and write basic English. You will also be tested on basic U.S. history and civics from the 100 questions covered in Section II.

For some candidates, this portion of the citizenship exam can be very stressful. Listening carefully and clearly understanding words can be difficult if English is not your first language. Here are three ways to boost your listening skills, which will help you to hear and understand English.

- **Listen closely and quietly**—to the radio, to the television, and to others that you meet during the course of the day. Try repeating silently to yourself the phrases they say. Notice when you remember a phrase correctly and when you don't.
- **Find role models**—listen carefully to radio and television newscasters, talk show hosts, members of the clergy, and others who are effective speakers. Try writing down a sentence that they say. Did you get it right or wrong?
- **Keep a journal**—include words and phrases that give you trouble. Practice saying them aloud and writing them down.

Active listening is a way of showing a speaker that you really hear what he or she is saying. When you listen actively, you get the information that you need and are able to provide the speaker with valuable feedback.

How to Listen Actively

- Pay attention
- Nod your head up and down at the speaker
- Use verbal confirmation, such as saying, "I see"
- Make eye contact

100 Questions

Your interviewer will ask you **ten** U.S. history and civics questions from the list of 100 questions. You must answer **six** of these questions correctly to pass. Go back and review Section II to study the 100 questions.

Repeat the main idea of the question at the beginning of your answer. This shows the interviewer that you understand the question. Plus, it gives you some time to think while you frame your answer.

For example, if the interviewer asks, "Which U.S. president ended slavery?" you could answer, "The U.S. president who ended slavery was Abraham Lincoln."

Here is an example of how this portion of the interview could proceed:

Interviewer: Now I'm going to ask you some questions about U.S. history and government.

Q: Which president is called the "father of our country"?

A: _____

Q: What is the Constitution?

A: _____

Q: Who is the vice president of the United States now?

A: _____

Q: There were 13 original states. Name one.

A: _____

Q: What did the Emancipation Proclamation do?

A: _____

Q: Name one state that borders Canada.

A: _____

Q: What major event occurred on September 11, 2001?

A: _____

Q: When do we celebrate Independence Day?

A: _____

Q: Where is the Statue of Liberty located?

A: _____

Q: What is the capital of your state?

A: _____

Dictation

The interviewer will read you one sentence, probably from the list of reading and dictation sentences listed on pages 152–153, and he or she will ask you to write it down on the provided paper. The sentence is usually repeated at least three times. Remember to listen carefully and ask your interviewer to repeat the sentence if you do not hear it well.

Interviewer: Now I'd like you to write the sentence that I say.
A senator is elected for six years.

What you do: Write the sentence!

_____

Reading

Next, the interviewer will show you a sentence and ask you to read it out loud. Practice reading from the list of sentences on pages 152–153. (These sentences are taken from the USCIS website, www.uscis.gov/civicsflashcards.)

Interviewer: I'm going to show you a sentence now. Read it out loud.
There are three branches of government.

What you do: Read it out loud!

Sample Reading and Dictation Sentences

Civics/History

A governor is the head executive of a state.

A senator is elected for six years.

All people want to be free.

All U.S. citizens have the right to vote.

America is the home of the brave.

America is the land of freedom.

America is the land of the free.

An amendment is a change to the Constitution.

Barack Obama is the president of the United States.

Citizens have the right to vote.

Congress is part of the American government.

Congress meets in Washington, D.C.

Congress passes laws in the United States.

George Washington is known as the "father of our country."

George Washington was the first president.

I love America.

Independence Day is a very important holiday.

I want to be a citizen because I love America.

I want to be a citizen of the United States.

I want to be an American citizen.

I want to become an American so I can vote.

It is important for all citizens to vote.

Joe Biden is the vice president of the United States.

Many people come to America for freedom.

Many people have died for freedom.

Martha Washington was the first First Lady.

Martin Luther King Jr. Day is an American holiday.

Only Congress can declare war.

Our government is divided into three branches.

People in America have the right to freedom.

People vote for the president in November.

Rhode Island was one of the 13 colonies.

Texas borders Mexico.

Thanksgiving is celebrated in November.

The American flag has stars and stripes.

The American flag has 13 stripes.

The Bill of Rights guarantees the freedom of speech.

The cabinet advises the president

The capital of the United States is Washington, D.C.

The colors of the flag are red, white, and blue.

The Constitution is the supreme law of our land.

The flag of the United States has 50 stars.

The House and Senate are parts of Congress.

The judicial branch interprets the laws.

The judicial branch reviews and interprets laws

The people have a voice in government.

The people in the class took a citizenship test.

The president enforces the laws.

The president has the power of veto.

The president is elected every four years.

The president lives in the White House.

The president lives in Washington, D.C.

The president must be an American citizen.

The president must be born in the United States.

The president signs bills into law.

The stars of the American flag are white.

The Statue of Liberty was a gift from France.

The stripes of the American flag are red and white.

The Supreme Court has a chief justice

The White House is in Washington, D.C.

The United States is the second largest country in North America.

The United States has five territories.

The United States of America has 50 states.

There are 50 states in the union.

There are three branches of government.

Everyday Life

He came to live with his brother.

He has a very big dog.

She knows how to ride a bike.

He wanted to find a job.

She wanted to talk to her boss.

He went to the post office.

His wife is at work right now.

His wife worked in the house.

I am too busy to talk today.

I bought a blue car today.

I came to ─────── (city) today for my interview.

I count the cars as they pass by the office.

I drive a blue car to work.

I go to work every day.

I have three children.

I know how to speak English.

I like to celebrate on holidays

I like to live in America.

I live in the state of ———————————.

I want to be a U.S. citizen.

It is a good job to start with.

My car does not work.

She can speak English very well.

She cooks for her friends.

She is my daughter, and he is my son.

He needs to buy some new clothes.

He wanted to live near his brother.

She lives in California.

She was happy with her house.

The boy threw a ball.

The children bought a newspaper.

The children play at school.

The children wanted a television.

The governor of my state is _____.

The man wanted to get a job.

The teacher was proud of her class.

The red house has a big tree.

They are a very happy family.

They are very happy with their car.

They buy many things at the store.

They came to live in the United States.

They go to the grocery store.

They have horses on their farm.

They live together in a big house.

They work well together.

Today, I am going to the store.

Today is a sunny day.

Warm clothing was on sale in the store.

We have a very clean house.

You cook very well.

You drink too much coffee.

You work very hard at your job.

Vocabulary Lists

The USCIS has developed vocabulary lists for the reading and dictation portions of the U.S. Citizenship Exam. In the list below, you will find the words that are found in the reading and dictation portions of the exam. Notice that the content focuses on civics and history. In addition to studying the sample reading and dictation sentences on the previous pages, becoming familiar with the words on this list will make it easier for you to understand the sentences that you will be asked to read and write during the exam.

People

Abraham Lincoln

George Washington

John Adams

Civics

American flag

American Indians

Bill of Rights

capital

citizen/citizens

city

Civil War

Congress

country

Father of Our Country

flag

free

freedom of speech

government

president

right

senators

state/states

White House

Places

Alaska

America

California
Canada
Delaware
Mexico
New York City
U.S.
United States
Washington, D.C.

Holidays
Columbus Day
Flag Day
Independence Day
Labor Day
Memorial Day
Presidents' Day
Thanksgiving

Months
February
May
June
July
September
October
November

Questions Words
how
what
when
where
who
why

Verbs
can
come
do/does
elect/elects
have/has

is/are/was/be
lives/lived
meet/meets
name
pay
vote
want

Other (Function)
a
and
during
for
here
in
of
on
the
to
we

Other (Content)
29
blue
colors
dollar bill
fifty/50
first
largest
many
most
north
one
one hundred/100
people
red
second
south
taxes
white

SECTION REVIEW

Remember the three useful phrases, and be sure that you can answer all of the following questions. Review this section if you need help.

Useful Phrases

- Please repeat that.
- Please speak more slowly.
- Please speak louder.

Greetings and Small Talk

- How are you?
- What is the weather like today? / How is the weather?
- What did you have for breakfast this morning?
- How did you get here today? / Who came with you?
- What day of the week is today?
- Do you know why you are here today?
- Why do you want to be a U.S. citizen?
- Do you have any questions before we begin?
- Have you studied for the citizenship test? What did you do?

Time Questions

- When did you first come to the United States?
- How long have you been a permanent resident?
- When was your last trip out of the United States?
- How long were you gone?
- How long have you lived at (current address)?
- How long have you worked at (current job)?

Place Questions

- Where did you first enter the United States? / What is your port of entry?
- What is your country of nationality?
- What is your country of birth? / Where were you born?

Have You Ever Questions

- **Have you ever** failed to file a tax return?
- **Have you ever** been part of the communist party / a terrorist organization?
- **Have you ever** been arrested, indicted, or convicted of a crime?

Another way to categorize these questions is by question word. Listen carefully to the first word of each question and the key words in the question. Ask your interviewer to repeat the question if you did not hear it the first time.

"What" Questions

- **What** is your name?
- **What** is your Social Security number?
- **What** is your home telephone number?
- **What** is your date of birth?
- **What** is your marital status?
- **What** is your nationality?
- **What** is your height / weight / eye color / hair color?
- **What** is your address?
- **What** is your husband's / wife's name?
- **What** is his / her immigration status?

"How" Questions

- **How** are you?
- **How** is the weather?
- **How** did you get here?
- **How** do you spell your last name?

"How Long" Questions

- **How long** have you been a permanent resident?
- **How long** have you lived at (current address)?
- **How long** have you worked at (current job)?
- **How long** did the trip outside the United States last?
- **How long** have you been married?

"Where" Questions

- **Where** were you born?
- **Where** do you live?
- **Where** do you work?
- **Where** did you go (when you last left the United States)?
- **Where** were your children born?

"When" Questions

- **When** were you born?
- **When** did you come to the United States?
- **When** did you get your permanent resident card?
- **When** did you get married?
- **When** did your spouse become a citizen?
- **When** did you move to (current address)?
- **When** was your last trip outside the United States?
- **When** did you return?
- **When** were your children born?

"Why" Questions

- **Why** do you want to become a citizen?
- **Why** were you out of the country for six months or longer?
- **Why** did you get divorced?
- **Why** aren't you working?

APPENDIX A
SAMPLE N-400 APPLICATION

This appendix contains a copy of the most current N-400 "Application for Naturalization." You can practice filling it out, but this is not the real application. You can get the real application from an USCIS office near you or online at www.uscis.gov. Remember that USCIS changes the N-400 from time to time, so the one you fill out might look a bit different from the one in this appendix.

OMB No. 1615-0052; Expires 01/31/11

Department of Homeland Security
U.S Citizenship and Immigration Services

N-400 Application
for Naturalization

Print clearly or type your answers using CAPITAL letters. Failure to print clearly may delay your application. Use black ink.

Part 1. Your Name *(Person applying for naturalization)*

Write your USCIS A-Number here:

A

A. Your current legal name.

Family Name *(Last Name)*

Given Name *(First Name)*   Full Middle Name *(If applicable)*

B. Your name **exactly** as it appears on your Permanent Resident Card.

Family Name *(Last Name)*

Given Name *(First Name)*   Full Middle Name *(If applicable)*

C. If you have ever used other names, provide them below.

Family Name *(Last Name)*	Given Name *(First Name)*	Middle Name

D. Name change *(optional)*

Read the Instructions before you decide whether to change your name.

1. Would you like to legally change your name? ☐ Yes ☐ No

2. If "Yes," print the new name you would like to use. Do not use initials or abbreviations when writing your new name.

Family Name *(Last Name)*

Given Name *(First Name)*   Full Middle Name

For USCIS Use Only

Bar Code	Date Stamp
	Remarks

Action Block

Part 2. Information About Your Eligibility *(Check only one)*

I am at least 18 years old **AND**

A. ☐ I have been a lawful permanent resident of the United States for at least five years.

B. ☐ I have been a lawful permanent resident of the United States for at least three years, **and** I have been married to and living with the same U.S. citizen for the last three years, **and** my spouse has been a U.S. citizen for the last three years.

C. ☐ I am applying on the basis of qualifying military service.

D. ☐ Other *(Explain)* _____

Form N-400 (Rev. 04/05/10) Y

Part 3. Information About You

Write your USCIS A-Number here:
A

A. U.S. Social Security Number

B. Date of Birth *(mm/dd/yyyy)*

C. Date You Became a Permanent Resident *(mm/dd/yyyy)*

D. Country of Birth

E. Country of Nationality

F. Are either of your parents U.S. citizens? *(If yes, see instructions)* ☐ Yes ☐ No

G. What is your current marital status? ☐ Single, Never Married ☐ Married ☐ Divorced ☐ Widowed

☐ Marriage Annulled or Other *(Explain)* _____

H. Are you requesting a waiver of the English and/or U.S. History and Government requirements based on a disability or impairment and attaching Form N-648 with your application? ☐ Yes ☐ No

I. Are you requesting an accommodation to the naturalization process because of a disability or impairment? *(See instructions for some examples of accommodations.)* ☐ Yes ☐ No

If you answered "Yes," check the box below that applies:

☐ I am deaf or hearing impaired and need a sign language interpreter who uses the following language: _____

☐ I use a wheelchair.

☐ I am blind or sight impaired.

☐ I will need another type of accommodation. Explain: _____

_____

_____

Part 4. Addresses and Telephone Numbers

A. Home Address - Street Number and Name *(Do **not** write a P.O. Box in this space.)*   Apartment Number

City   County   State   ZIP Code   Country

B. Care of   Mailing Address - Street Number and Name *(If different from home address)*   Apartment Number

City   State   ZIP Code   Country

C. Daytime Phone Number *(If any)*   Evening Phone Number *(If any)*   E-Mail Address *(If any)*

(   )   (   )

SAMPLE

Part 5. Information for Criminal Records Search	Write your USCIS A-Number here: A

NOTE: The categories below are those required by the FBI. See instructions for more information.

A. Gender

☐ Male   ☐ Female

B. Height

Feet	Inches

C. Weight

Pounds

D. Are you Hispanic or Latino?   ☐ Yes   ☐ No

E. Race *(Select one or more)*

☐ White   ☐ Asian   ☐ Black or African American   ☐ American Indian or Alaskan Native   ☐ Native Hawaiian or Other Pacific Islander

F. Hair color

☐ Black   ☐ Brown   ☐ Blonde   ☐ Gray   ☐ White   ☐ Red   ☐ Sandy   ☐ Bald (No Hair)

G. Eye color

☐ Brown   ☐ Blue   ☐ Green   ☐ Hazel   ☐ Gray   ☐ Black   ☐ Pink   ☐ Maroon   ☐ Other

Part 6. Information About Your Residence and Employment

A. Where have you lived during the last five years? Begin with where you live now and then list every place you lived for the last five years. If you need more space, use a separate sheet of paper.

Street Number and Name, Apartment Number, City, State, Zip Code, and Country	Dates *(mm/dd/yyyy)*	
	From	To
Current Home Address - Same as Part 4.A		Present

B. Where have you worked (or, if you were a student, what schools did you attend) during the last five years? Include military service. Begin with your current or latest employer and then list every place you have worked or studied for the last five years. If you need more space, use a separate sheet of paper.

Employer or School Name	Employer or School Address *(Street, City, and State)*	Dates *(mm/dd/yyyy)*		Your Occupation
		From	To	

Part 7. Time Outside the United States
(Including Trips to Canada, Mexico and the Caribbean Islands)

Write your USCIS A-Number here:
A

A. How many total days did you spend outside of the United States during the past five years? [   ] days

B. How many trips of 24 hours or more have you taken outside of the United States during the past five years? [   ] trips

C. List below all the trips of 24 hours or more that you have taken outside of the United States since becoming a lawful permanent resident. Begin with your most recent trip. If you need more space, use a separate sheet of paper.

Date You Left the United States *(mm/dd/yyyy)*	Date You Returned to the United States *(mm/dd/yyyy)*	Did Trip Last Six Months or More?	Countries to Which You Traveled	Total Days Out of the United States
		☐ Yes ☐ No		
		☐ Yes ☐ No		
		☐ Yes ☐ No		
		☐ Yes ☐ No		
		☐ Yes ☐ No		
		☐ Yes ☐ No		
		☐ Yes ☐ No		
		☐ Yes ☐ No		
		☐ Yes ☐ No		
		☐ Yes ☐ No		

Part 8. Information About Your Marital History

A. How many times have you been married (including annulled marriages)? [   ] If you have **never** been married, go to Part 9.

B. If you are now married, give the following information about your spouse:

1. Spouse's Family Name *(Last Name)*   Given Name *(First Name)*   Full Middle Name *(If applicable)*

2. Date of Birth *(mm/dd/yyyy)*   **3.** Date of Marriage *(mm/dd/yyyy)*   **4.** Spouse's U.S. Social Security #

5. Home Address - Street Number and Name   Apartment Number

City   State   Zip Code

Part 8. **Information About Your Marital History** (*Continued*)	Write your USCIS A-Number here: A

C. Is your spouse a U.S. citizen? ☐ Yes ☐ No

D. If your spouse is a U.S. citizen, give the following information:

    1. When did your spouse become a U.S. citizen? ☐ At Birth ☐ Other

    If "Other," give the following information:

    2. Date your spouse became a U.S. citizen

    3. Place your spouse became a U.S. citizen (*See instructions*)

    City and State

E. If your spouse is **not** a U.S. citizen, give the following information :

    1. Spouse's Country of Citizenship

    2. Spouse's USCIS A- Number (*If applicable*)   A

    3. Spouse's Immigration Status

    ☐ Lawful Permanent Resident   ☐ Other

F. If you were married before, provide the following information about your prior spouse. If you have more than one previous marriage, use a separate sheet of paper to provide the information requested in Questions 1-5 below.

    1. Prior Spouse's Family Name (*Last Name*)   Given Name (*First Name*)   Full Middle Name (*If applicable*)

    2. Prior Spouse's Immigration Status

    ☐ U.S. Citizen

    ☐ Lawful Permanent Resident

    ☐ Other

    3. Date of Marriage (*mm/dd/yyyy*)

    4. Date Marriage Ended (*mm/dd/yyyy*)

    5. How Marriage Ended

    ☐ Divorce   ☐ Spouse Died   ☐ Other

G. How many times has your current spouse been married (including annulled marriages)?

If your spouse has **ever** been married before, give the following information about **your spouse's** prior marriage.
If your spouse has more than one previous marriage, use a separate sheet(s) of paper to provide the information requested in Questions 1 - 5 below.

    1. Prior Spouse's Family Name (*Last Name*)   Given Name (*First Name*)   Full Middle Name (*If applicable*)

    2. Prior Spouse's Immigration Status

    ☐ U.S. Citizen

    ☐ Lawful Permanent Resident

    ☐ Other

    3. Date of Marriage (*mm/dd/yyyy*)

    4. Date Marriage Ended (*mm/dd/yyyy*)

    5. How Marriage Ended

    ☐ Divorce   ☐ Spouse Died   ☐ Other

SAMPLE

Part 9. Information About Your Children	Write your USCIS A-Number here: A

A. How many sons and daughters have you had? For more information on which sons and daughters you should include and how to complete this section, see the Instructions.

B. Provide the following information about all of your sons and daughters. If you need more space, use a separate sheet of paper.

Full Name of Son or Daughter	Date of Birth (mm/dd/yyyy)	USCIS A- number (if child has one)	Country of Birth	Current Address (Street, City, State and Country)
		A		
		A		
		A		
		A		
		A		
		A		
		A		
		A		

Add Children   Go to continuation page

Part 10. Additional Questions

Answer Questions 1 through 14. If you answer "Yes" to any of these questions, include a written explanation with this form. Your written explanation should (1) explain why your answer was "Yes" and (2) provide any additional information that helps to explain your answer.

A. General Questions.

1. Have you **ever** claimed to be a U.S. citizen *(in writing or any other way)*? ☐ Yes ☐ No

2. Have you **ever** registered to vote in any Federal, State, or local election in the United States? ☐ Yes ☐ No

3. Have you **ever** voted in any Federal, State, or local election in the United States? ☐ Yes ☐ No

4. Since becoming a lawful permanent resident, have you **ever** failed to file a required Federal, State, or local tax return? ☐ Yes ☐ No

5. Do you owe any Federal, State, or local taxes that are overdue? ☐ Yes ☐ No

6. Do you have any title of nobility in any foreign country? ☐ Yes ☐ No

7. Have you ever been declared legally incompetent or been confined to a mental institution within the last five years? ☐ Yes ☐ No

Form N-400 (Rev. 04/05/10) Y Page 6

Part 10. Additional Questions (*Continued*)	Write your USCIS A-Number here: A

B. Affiliations.

8. a Have you **ever** been a member of or associated with any organization, association, fund foundation, party, club, society, or similar group in the United States or in any other place? ☐ Yes ☐ No

  b. If you answered "Yes," list the name of each group below. If you need more space, attach the names of the other group(s) on a separate sheet of paper.

Name of Group	Name of Group
1.	6.
2.	7.
3.	8.
4.	9.
5.	10.

9. Have you **ever** been a member of or in any way associated (*either directly or indirectly*) with:

  a. The Communist Party? ☐ Yes ☐ No

  b. Any other totalitarian party? ☐ Yes ☐ No

  c. A terrorist organization? ☐ Yes ☐ No

10. Have you **ever** advocated (*either directly or indirectly*) the overthrow of any government by force or violence? ☐ Yes ☐ No

11. Have you **ever** persecuted (*either directly or indirectly*) any person because of race, religion, national origin, membership in a particular social group, or political opinion? ☐ Yes ☐ No

12. Between March 23, 1933, and May 8, 1945, did you work for or associate in any way (*either directly or indirectly*) with:

  a. The Nazi government of Germany? ☐ Yes ☐ No

  b. Any government in any area (1) occupied by, (2) allied with, or (3) established with the help of the Nazi government of Germany? ☐ Yes ☐ No

  c. Any German, Nazi, or S.S. military unit, paramilitary unit, self-defense unit, vigilante unit, citizen unit, police unit, government agency or office, extermination camp, concentration camp, prisoner of war camp, prison, labor camp, or transit camp? ☐ Yes ☐ No

C. Continuous Residence.

Since becoming a lawful permanent resident of the United States:

13. Have you **ever** called yourself a "nonresident" on a Federal, State, or local tax return? ☐ Yes ☐ No

14. Have you **ever** failed to file a Federal, State, or local tax return because you considered yourself to be a "nonresident"? ☐ Yes ☐ No

Part 10. Additional Questions *(continued)*	Write your USCIS A-Number here: A

D. Good Moral Character.

For the purposes of this application, you must answer "Yes" to the following questions, if applicable, even if your records were sealed or otherwise cleared or if anyone, including a judge, law enforcement officer, or attorney, told you that you no longer have a record.

15. Have you **ever** committed a crime or offense for which you were **not** arrested? ☐ Yes ☐ No

16. Have you **ever** been arrested, cited, or detained by any law enforcement officer (including USCIS or former INS and military officers) for any reason? ☐ Yes ☐ No

17. Have you **ever** been charged with committing any crime or offense? ☐ Yes ☐ No

18. Have you **ever** been convicted of a crime or offense? ☐ Yes ☐ No

19. Have you **ever** been placed in an alternative sentencing or a rehabilitative program (for example: diversion, deferred prosecution, withheld adjudication, deferred adjudication)? ☐ Yes ☐ No

20. Have you **ever** received a suspended sentence, been placed on probation, or been paroled? ☐ Yes ☐ No

21. Have you **ever** been in jail or prison? ☐ Yes ☐ No

If you answered "Yes" to any of Questions 15 through 21, complete the following table. If you need more space, use a separate sheet of paper to give the same information.

Why were you arrested, cited, detained, or charged?	Date arrested, cited, detained, or charged? *(mm/dd/yyyy)*	Where were you arrested, cited, detained, or charged? *(City, State, Country)*	Outcome or disposition of the arrest, citation, detention, or charge *(No charges filed, charges dismissed, jail, probation, etc.)*

Answer Questions 22 through 33. If you answer "Yes" to any of these questions, attach (1) your written explanation why your answer was "Yes" and (2) any additional information or documentation that helps explain your answer.

22. Have you **ever**:

    a. Been a habitual drunkard? ☐ Yes ☐ No

    b. Been a prostitute, or procured anyone for prostitution? ☐ Yes ☐ No

    c. Sold or smuggled controlled substances, illegal drugs, or narcotics? ☐ Yes ☐ No

    d. Been married to more than one person at the same time? ☐ Yes ☐ No

    e. Helped anyone enter or try to enter the United States illegally? ☐ Yes ☐ No

    f. Gambled illegally or received income from illegal gambling? ☐ Yes ☐ No

    g. Failed to support your dependents or to pay alimony? ☐ Yes ☐ No

23. Have you **ever** given false or misleading information to any U.S. Government official while applying for any immigration benefit or to prevent deportation, exclusion, or removal? ☐ Yes ☐ No

24. Have you **ever** lied to any U.S. Government official to gain entry or admission into the United States? ☐ Yes ☐ No

Part 10. Additional Questions *(Continued)*	Write your USCIS A-Number here: A

E. Removal, Exclusion, and Deportation Proceedings.

25. Are removal, exclusion, rescission, or deportation proceedings pending against you? ☐ Yes ☐ No

26. Have you **ever** been removed, excluded, or deported from the United States? ☐ Yes ☐ No

27. Have you **ever** been ordered to be removed, excluded, or deported from the United States? ☐ Yes ☐ No

28. Have you **ever** applied for any kind of relief from removal, exclusion, or deportation? ☐ Yes ☐ No

F. Military Service.

29. Have you **ever** served in the U.S. Armed Forces? ☐ Yes ☐ No

30. Have you **ever** left the United States to avoid being drafted into the U.S. Armed Forces? ☐ Yes ☐ No

31. Have you **ever** applied for any kind of exemption from military service in the U.S. Armed Forces? ☐ Yes ☐ No

32. Have you **ever** deserted from the U.S. Armed Forces? ☐ Yes ☐ No

G. Selective Service Registration.

33. Are you a male who lived in the United States at any time between your 18th and 26th birthdays in any status except as a lawful nonimmigrant? ☐ Yes ☐ No

If you answered "NO," go on to question 34.

If you answered "YES," provide the information below.

If you answered "YES," but you did not register with the Selective Service System and are still under 26 years of age, you must register before you apply for naturalization, so that you can complete the information below:

Date Registered (mm/dd/yyyy) [   ]   Selective Service Number [   ]

If you answered "YES," but you did not register with the Selective Service and you are now 26 years old or older, attach a statement explaining why you did not register.

H. Oath Requirements. *(See Part 14 for the text of the oath)*

Answer Questions 34 through 39. If you answer "No" to any of these questions, attach (1) your written explanation why the answer was "No" and (2) any additional information or documentation that helps to explain your answer.

34. Do you support the Constitution and form of government of the United States? ☐ Yes ☐ No

35. Do you understand the full Oath of Allegiance to the United States? ☐ Yes ☐ No

36. Are you willing to take the full Oath of Allegiance to the United States? ☐ Yes ☐ No

37. If the law requires it, are you willing to bear arms on behalf of the United States? ☐ Yes ☐ No

38. If the law requires it, are you willing to perform noncombatant services in the U.S. Armed Forces? ☐ Yes ☐ No

39. If the law requires it, are you willing to perform work of national importance under civilian direction? ☐ Yes ☐ No

Form N-400 (Rev. 04/05/10) Y Page 9

Part 11. Your Signature

Write your USCIS A-Number here:
A

I certify, under penalty of perjury under the laws of the United States of America, that this application, and the evidence submitted with it, are all true and correct. I authorize the release of any information that the USCIS needs to determine my eligibility for naturalization.

Your Signature

Date *(mm/dd/yyyy)*

Part 12. Signature of Person Who Prepared This Application for You *(If applicable)*

I declare under penalty of perjury that I prepared this application at the request of the above person. The answers provided are based on information of which I have personal knowledge and/or were provided to me by the above named person in response to the *exact questions* contained on this form.

Preparer's Printed Name

Preparer's Signature

Date *(mm/dd/yyyy)*

Preparer's Firm or Organization Name *(If applicable)*

Preparer's Daytime Phone Number

Preparer's Address - Street Number and Name

City

State

Zip Code

NOTE: Do not complete Parts 13 and 14 until a USCIS Officer instructs you to do so.

Part 13. Signature at Interview

I swear (affirm) and certify under penalty of perjury under the laws of the United States of America that I know that the contents of this application for naturalization subscribed by me, including corrections numbered 1 through _____ and the evidence submitted by me numbered pages 1 through _____ , are true and correct to the best of my knowledge and belief.

Subscribed to and sworn to (affirmed) before me

Officer's Printed Name or Stamp

Date *(mm/dd/yyyy)*

Complete Signature of Applicant

Officer's Signature

Part 14. Oath of Allegiance

If your application is approved, you will be scheduled for a public oath ceremony at which time you will be required to take the following Oath of Allegiance immediately prior to becoming a naturalized citizen. By signing, you acknowledge your willingness and ability to take this oath:

I hereby declare, on oath, that I absolutely and entirely renounce and abjure all allegiance and fidelity to any foreign prince, potentate, state, or sovereignty, of whom or which I have heretofore been a subject or citizen;

that I will support and defend the Constitution and laws of the United States of America against all enemies, foreign and domestic;

that I will bear true faith and allegiance to the same;

that I will bear arms on behalf of the United States when required by the law;

that I will perform noncombatant service in the Armed Forces of the United States when required by the law;

that I will perform work of national importance under civilian direction when required by the law; and

that I take this obligation freely, without any mental reservation or purpose of evasion, so help me God.

Printed Name of Applicant

Complete Signature of Applicant

APPENDIX B
ONLINE AND
PRINT RESOURCES

The Internet can be a valuable learning and research tool. Here is a list of websites that can supplement your studies:

Ben's Guide to U.S. Government for Kids
www.bensguide.gpo.gov

Library of Congress
www.loc.gov

Encyclopedia Britannica Online
www.britannica.com

Our Courts
www.ourcourts.org

History Channel Online
www.history.com

Project Constitution
www.projectconstitution.org

History.org
www.ushistory.org

USCIS Online
www.uscis.gov/citizenshiptest

iCivics
www.icivics.org

The White House Online
www.whitehouse.gov

There are many books about U.S. history and civics that can assist you with learning about the United States. You can visit your local library or bookstore to look up titles related to specific topics that you need to study, or general history or civics. To start, here is a list of books that will give you a greater understanding of American history and a better idea of how the country works.

Twenty-Five Lessons in Citizenship, by D.L. Hennessey and Lenore Hennessey Richardson (D.L. Hennessey, 1997)

The Complete Idiot's Guide to U.S. Government and Politics, by Franco Scardino (Alpha Books, 2009)

The U.S. Constitution: And Fascinating Facts about It, by Terry L. Jordan (Oak Hill Publishing, 1999)

A People's History of the United States: 1492–Present, by Howard Zinn (Harper Perennial Modern Classics, 2005)

History of the United States, by Charles Austin Beard (General Books, 2009)

The United States: A Brief Narrative History, by Link Hullar and Scott Nelson (Harlan Davidson, 2006)

A Documentary History of the United States: 8th edition, by Richard D. Hefner (Signet, 2009)

U.S. History for Dummies: 2nd edition, by Steve Wiegand (For Dummies, 2009)

The Everything American Government Book, by Nick Ragone (Adams Media, 2004)

Notes

Notes

Notes

Notes

Notes

Notes

Notes

Notes

Notes

Notes

Notes

Notes